THE EPISTLE
TO THE GALATIANS

A Study Manual

by
FLOYD E. HAMILTON

BAKER BOOK HOUSE
Grand Rapids 6, Michigan

ISBN: 0-8010-4050-7

First Printing, March 1959
Second Printing, September 1968
Third Printing, June 1972

Printed in the United States of America

Dedicated to
My Children

TABLE OF CONTENTS

THE PURPOSE OF THIS MANUAL

This Manual is written for a very definite purpose. It is a *Study Manual* for the EPISTLE TO THE GALATIANS. It does not pretend to be a commentary in the usual sense of the word, for little attempt is made to give conflicting views of the meaning of important words and phrases, except in the discussion of such basic matters as the North and South Galatian theories and the various visits of Paul to Jerusalem. The principal emphasis of this Study Manual is on the Outline of the Epistle. It is therefore unusually elaborate and detailed. Only when the purpose of the epistle and the argument of Paul as a whole are clearly understood can one teach or study it profitably in the classroom, or preach effectively on the great themes of the epistle. Devotional study of this great epistle can be most helpful when the central purpose and reasoning of the apostle are thoroughly understood. Once the general purpose and discussion of the book are grasped, detailed study of it will be more profitable. Though the "bones of exegesis" from the original Greek will not always be clearly seen, the Greek text has been thoroughly studied in the preparation of this study manual. The following commentaries on Galatians can be profitably studied:

J. B. Lightfoot: "The Epistle of St. Paul to the Galatians" *Classic Commentary Library* (reprint) (Zondervan) 1957.

H. A. W. Meyer: *"Galatians and Ephesians."* Translated from the 5th edition by G. H. Venables (Funk and Wagnalls) 1884.

J. Gresham Machen: "Notes on Biblical Exposition" (Galatians) in *Christianity Today,* 1931-1932.

C. J. Ellicott: "Epistle to the Galatians" in *"The Epistles of Saint Paul"* (W. H. Halliday) 1872.

P. E. Huxtable: "Galatians" in *The Pulpit Commentary* (Funk and Wagnalls) 1907.

E. DeWitt Burton: "The Epistle to the Galatians" in the *International Critical Commentary* (T. and T. Clark) 1950.

Lehman Strauss: *Galatians and Ephesians* (Loizeaux) 1957.

C. H. Irwin: "Galatians" in *Bible Commentary* (John C. Winston) 1928.

Jamieson, Fausset and Brown: "Galatians" in *Commentary on the Whole Bible* (Zondervan) 1934.

INTRODUCTION

THE AUTHOR. Galatians is one of the few books in the New Testament regarding which there has been comparatively little discussion about the author. It is almost universally agreed that the Apostle Paul was the author. The historical facts given in the epistle, the style and the theme of the book all fit the assumption that Paul was the author as the first word in the epistle declares. The external evidence overwhelmingly supports this view.

THE PLACE OF WRITING. The majority of modern scholars believe that the epistle was written during Paul's lengthy stay in Ephesus, during the third missionary journey. I am inclined, however, to agree with Lightfoot that the book was probably written just after II Corinthians, either on the journey through Macedonia to Corinth, or after reaching Corinth, but before the writing of the Epistle to the Romans at Corinth. The close similarity in many respects of the thought of Galatians and Romans seems to indicate that they come from the same period in Paul's life. Moreover the almost total absence of any indication in II Corinthians that Paul was then troubled by the problem of the Judaizers, seems to point to the writing of Galatians after the writing of II Corinthians, and just after his receiving news of the activity of the Judaizers in the Galatian churches.

THE DATE OF THE WRITING OF GALATIANS. If Corinth was the place where Galatians was written, then we can pinpoint the date with fair accuracy as being at the close of A.D. 57 or early in 58. The advocates of the South Galatian theory usually date the epistle as early as A.D. 54, and many who accept the North Galatian theory date it early in the three year Ephesian residence, in A.D. 56 or 57. The Textus Receptus has a subscription, "To the Galatians, written from Rome." In such a case, of course it would have to have been written during the first Roman imprisonment, in A.D. 59 to A.D. 62, but this seems unlikely in view of all the evidence.

THE GALATIANS. Critics have been divided regarding the identity of the recipients of this epistle. Many people have held that the Galatians were the people of the churches in Derbe, Lystra, Iconium and Antioch, in South Galatia. Paul established these churches on the first missionary journey. The weight of the evidence, however, seems to be in favor of the North Galatian theory. During the second missionary journey we are told that "they went through the region of Phrygia and Galatia,

having been forbidden of the Holy Spirit to speak the word in
Asia" (Acts 16:6) . In the first verses of chapter 16, it is implied
that after going to Derbe, where he circumcised Timothy, and
Lystra and Iconium, he *then* went through the region of Phrygia
and Galatia (Acts 16:6) .

The second mention of Galatia is in Acts 18:23, on the third
missionary journey. "And having spent some time there [at
Antioch in Syria] he departed, and went through the region of
Galatia and Phrygia in order, establishing the churches." The
phrase "in order" is held by the advocates of the South Galatian
theory to indicate that he started in Derbe, and then went to
Lystra, Iconium and Antioch in that order before going on to
Ephesus. Timothy, Paul's companion, was a native of Derbe,
and would naturally be anxious to revisit his mother and grandmother. However, in view of the popular designation of Derbe
and Lystra as Lycaonian cities (Acts 14:6) , and of Antioch and
Iconium as cities of Pisidia (Acts 13:14) , it seems more probable that North Galatia is meant in Acts 16:6. While Timothy
would naturally want to visit his mother and grandmother in
Derbe, those churches had been revisited on the second missionary journey, and seem to have been prospering, while the
churches in North Galatia (if they were established on the
second journey) needed all the encouragement they could get.
Paul, therefore, might have gone directly north from Tarsus, to
Ancyra, the capital of Galatia, and thence down through Phrygia,
either by-passing Iconium and Lystra and Derbe, to Ephesus, or
have made a quick trip down through those cities before going
to Ephesus. It is possible too that Timothy did not join Paul
until Paul reached Ephesus, for Paul used him as a messenger
later (Acts 19:22) . Paul might have sent him from Tarsus to
his home in Derbe, to report on the churches in Lycaonia and
Pisidia as well as to strengthen them, while he himself went
directly to Ephesus from Galatia and Phrygia. The term "Galatia" at that time was more applicable to the regions in the
north where the Galatians dwelt rather than to the southern
region which did not become a part of the Roman province of
Galatia until later. Apparently when Paul first visited them he
became sick with or concerned about the malady from which he
prayed to be cured (Gal. 4:14-15, and II Cor. 12:8-9) .

The similarity of the contents of Galatians to the contents of
Romans places both epistles close to each other in time of
writing, and renders the early date of the Galatians epistle less
likely.

THE PURPOSE AND THEME OF THE EPISTLE. The theme of the Epistle to the Galatians is similar to the theme of Romans: justification by faith alone, apart from works of the law (Gal. 3:11). The purpose of the epistle was to defend Paul's apostolic authority and to expound and defend the gospel of justification by faith alone. Men from Jerusalem, or possibly local Jewish Christians, whom we call Judaizers, were seeking to undermine Paul's apostolic authority and to bring the Galatian Christians under the bondage of the Mosaic Law, by forcing them to become circumcised. The Galatian Christians were apparently being carried away by their teachings, and were ceasing to trust in Christ alone for salvation. This called forth the severe condemnation and rebukes of the epistle.

OUTLINE OF THE EPISTLE TO THE GALATIANS

INTRODUCTION (1:1-10)

A. The Address (1:1-5)
   1. The Salutation (1:1,2)
   2. The Greeting (1:3)
   3. The Plan of Redemption (1:4)
   4. Praise to God (1:5)

B. The Occasion of the Epistle (1:6-10)
   1. The Apostasy of the Galatians (1:6,7)
   2. The Preaching of a Different Gospel (1:8,9)
   3. The Accusation that Paul Was a Man-Pleaser (1:10)

I. *PAUL DEFENDS HIS APOSTOLIC AUTHORITY* (1:11–2:21)

A. The Source of Paul's Apostleship: Christ, Not Men (1:11, 12)

B. Vindication of Paul's Apostolic Authority: Paul's Personal History (1:13–2:21)
   1. Paul before Conversion a Persecutor of Christians (1:13,14)
   2. Paul's Conversion (1:15,16a)
   3. Paul after Conversion (1:16b–2:21)
      a. Shows Himself Not Dependent on Other Apostles (1:16b-24)
      b. Recognized in Conference with Other Disciples as Already Chosen by God to Be an Apostle (2:1-10)
      c. Shows by Rebuking Peter at Antioch that He Is Not Inferior to Peter or the Other Disciples (2:11-21)
         (1) Peter's Hypocrisy at Antioch Caused Paul to Rebuke Him Publicly (2:11-14a)
         (2) The Rebuke Was an Exposition of the Gospel Paul Preached (2:14b-21)

II. *PAUL DEFENDS HIS GOSPEL* (3:1–4:31)

A. An Argument from Experience (3:1-5)
   The Galatians Received the Spirit through Faith, Not Works of the Law (3:1-5)

B. The Argument from Scripture (3:6-22)
   1. Abraham Was Justified by Faith, Not Works of the Law (3:6)

INTRODUCTION (1:1-10)

A. The Address (1:1-5)

1. The Salutation (1:1,2)

a. **(1:1)** *"Paul, an apostle, (not from men nor through man, but through Jesus Christ, and God the Father, who raised him from the dead)."* Paul defends his apostleship by stating that it came, not from or through a man but directly from Jesus Christ. His enemies, the Judaizers, who were disturbing the faith of the Galatians, charged that Paul was a second-rate apostle, much below the rank of the other apostles, like Peter, and that he had gotten his authority from them. In greeting the Galatians Paul declares his apostleship did not come *through* a man, but came directly from Jesus Christ. Here Paul sets Jesus Christ apart from the rest of humanity, and so emphasizes his deity that he seems to regard Christ's humanity as not sufficiently important to mention. Neither Paul nor the Judaizers challenged the deity of Christ. That was not the question at issue. The question in dispute was whether Paul received his authority from the divine Jesus Christ or from men like Peter, the apostle. Of course Paul knew that Jesus was both man and God, and so did the Judaizers.

b. **(1:2)** Paul's Co-workers. *"And all the brethren that are with me, unto the churches of Galatia."* Paul was not laboring alone. Probably Luke (Acts 20:6), Timothy, Erastus (Acts 19:22), and possibly Gaius, Tychicus and Trophimus, at least, were with· him when he wrote this epistle. Others joined him on the journey to Jerusalem (Acts 20:4). Possibly Titus was also with him, having brought news of conditions in the churches of Galatia. There was more than one church in Galatia.

2. The Greeting (1:3)

(1:3) *"Grace to you and peace from God the Father, and our Lord Jesus Christ."* The apostolic salutation is here given. Grace (unmerited favor) and peace (subjective, a matter of the heart, and objective, between man and God) are both from God the Father and from our Lord Jesus Christ. To call Jesus "Lord" was to ascribe deity to him, and to emphasize the fact that Christians are bondslaves of Christ.

3. The Plan of Redemption (1:4)

(1:4) *"Who gave himself for our sins, that he might deliver us out of this present evil world, according to the will of our God and Father."* The introduction to the epistle includes the plan of God to redeem the church through the voluntary death of Christ for the sins of his people. No one forced Christ to die in our place. That act was voluntary. It was, however, according to the will of God the Father.

4. Praise to God (1:5)

(1:5) *"To whom be the glory for ever and ever. Amen."* The address closes with an exclamation of praise to the glory of God. "Amen" means, "so be it." It is a statement of certainty.

B. The Occasion of the Epistle (1:6-10)

Lightfoot says, "The Apostle rebukes the Galatians for their apostasy, denounces the false teachers, and declares the eternal truth of the Gospel which he preached." Information had just reached Paul that Judaizers were attacking his authority in order to oppose successfully the gospel Paul preached of salvation by faith in Christ alone. Paul must defend his apostolic authority in order to defend the gospel.

1. The Apostasy of the Galatians (1:6-7)

a. **(1:6)** *"I marvel that ye are so quickly removing from him that called you in the grace of Christ unto a different gospel."* The Galatians have quickly deserted the gospel of salvation by faith alone and accepted a different teaching, salvation through faith and works, that is, obedience to the Mosaic ceremonial law, particularly circumcision as well as faith in the work of Christ. The word *heteron* which is here translated "another," is usually used of differences in kind.

b. **(1:7)** *"Which is not another gospel: only there are some that trouble you, and would pervert the gospel of Christ."* *Allo*, the original Greek word here translated "another," differs from *heteron*, by referring to a second resembling the first, as, "give me another apple (like the first one) ." Paul is saying that the teaching of the Judaizers is not another gospel which can be placed alongside of the true gospel as an alternate choice for belief, for there can be only one true gospel which Paul preached. Any opposing teaching is false.

2. The Preaching of a Different Gospel (1:8,9)

a. **(1:8)** *"But though we, or an angel from heaven, should*

*preach unto you any gospel other than that which we preached
unto you, let him be anathema."* A curse on those who preach a
different gospel, pretending that it is the truth, is pronounced.
No man nor angel from heaven could preach another *true*
gospel, if it was contrary to what Paul had preached. If the
Galatians are believing the teaching contrary to Paul's gospel,
they are believing falsehood, and there will be a curse on those
who preach it. But what is the "gospel of Christ?" Is it the
gospel which Christ preached? Or is it the "gospel preached
about Christ?" It is claimed by some modernists that Christ
preached a gospel of the fatherhood of God and the brotherhood of man, and that he did not present himself as the object
of faith. As we will later see Christ did not preach such a gospel.
Christ taught that he was the Messiah (John 4:26) ; he claimed
omnipotence (Matt. 28:18) ; he claimed to be the Son of God
(Luke 22:70) ; he claimed to forgive sin (Matt. 9:6). He
claimed that he had come to earth to "seek and to save that
which was lost" (Luke 19:10). He declared that the Son of
Man came "to give his life a ransom for many" (Matt. 20:28).
He declared that "he that believeth on the Son hath eternal
life; but he that obeyeth not the Son shall not see life, but the
wrath of God abideth on him" (John 3:36). He declared, "if
God were your father ye would love me: for I came forth and
am come from God; . . . Ye are of your father the devil" (John
8:42-44), in speaking to the Pharisees, which certainly does not
teach the universal fatherhood of God or the brotherhood of
man. The true gospel which Paul preached is the gospel *about*
Jesus Christ, that he was the pre-existent Son of God; that he
was incarnated in a human body; that he kept God's law sin-
lessly; that he died in the place of God's elect children, on the
cross; that he rose from the dead on the third day, ascended to
heaven, reigns in power now with the Father, and will come
again to judge the world at the last day. The true gospel declares that through belief and trust in Jesus Christ *alone* is
there eternal salvation.

b. (1:9) *"As we have said before, so say I now again, If any
man preacheth unto you any gospel other than that which you
received, let him be anathema."* In this ninth verse Paul repeats
the curse on those who preach a different gospel from the true
gospel which he preaches. The repeating of this curse gives
emphasis to Paul's thought.

3. The Accusation that Paul Was a Man-Pleaser (1:10)

(1:10) *"For am I now seeking .the favor of men, or of God?*

Or am I striving to please men? If I were still pleasing men, I should not be a servant of Christ." The Judaizers had charged that Paul was a man-pleaser, who taught circumcision when he was with the Jews, and sought to please the Gentiles by giving up the necessity of keeping the Mosaic Law when he was with the Gentiles. In verse 10 Paul points to his stern curse against those preaching a different teaching, as proof that he was concerned only with pleasing God, not man, even though it made enemies for him. If he sought to please men at the expense of the truth of the gospel, he would be a false "bondslave" of Christ. The "now" here refers specifically to the words Paul has just used in the preceding verses, cursing those who preached different teaching from the gospel.

I. *PAUL DEFENDS HIS APOSTOLIC AUTHORITY* (1:11—2:21)

A. The Source of Paul's Apostleship: Christ, Not Men (1:11,12)

1. **(1:11)** *"For I make known to you, brethren, as touching the gospel which was preached by me, that it is not after man."* The gospel did not come to Paul according to men, that is, it is not "of such a quality as it would be if it were the work of men" (Meyer). The expression "not *after* man" does not refer to the source of the gospel as much as its quality: it is not of human origin as shown by its nature. It is difficult to decide whether the verse should be introduced by "for" or "but," as the textual evidence is evenly divided. If "but" is accepted it would mean that the apostle resumes his argument interrupted by his personal defense.

2. **(1:12)** *"For neither did I receive it from man, nor was I taught it, but it came to me through revelation of Jesus Christ."* Paul here indicates that he was not taught the gospel by another apostle and did not receive it from any man, but received it by revelation from Christ, possibly while he was in Arabia. He did not receive the gospel through any intermediary.

B. Paul's Personal History Vindicates His Apostolic Authority (1:13—2:21)

1. Paul before Conversion a Persecutor of Christians (1:13;14)

a. **(1:13)** *"For ye have heard of my manner of life in time past in the Jews' religion, how that beyond measure I persecuted the church of God, and made havoc of it."* Paul could not have gotten his gospel from the Apostles while he was in Jerusalem, for he was then a persecutor of the Christian church. He here calls the church, "the church of God." He calls the whole body of Christians, "the church of God." The word ecclesia really means "assembly," and was used for any civil or political gathering of people. In Acts 19:32 the gathering of the mob was called *ecclesia*. The word was used in the Septuagint to refer to the solemn assembly of God's covenant people, while in the Christian usage it referred to (1) the individuals meeting in any house or building, (2) to all the Christians in a given city, though they might be meeting in separate places, or (3) to the whole universal body of Christians wherever found.

In this verse it apparently refers to the third usage and includes the whole body of Christians. Paul says he was trying to destroy the whole of Christianity.

b. (1:14) *"And I advanced in the Jews' religion beyond many of mine own age among my countrymen, being more exceedingly zealous for the traditions of my fathers."* The phrase "in my race," offers additional proof that Paul was addressing Gentile Christians, not primarily Jewish Christians. Paul characterizes himself as "being zealous more abundantly." He is saying that he belonged to the more extreme party of the Pharisees, who called themselves "zealots of the law, zealots of God." They were intense patriots and bitter opponents of Roman rule. This seems rather incongruous for Paul who was a Roman citizen, but perhaps that very fact led him to lean backwards in his zealous patriotism to defend himself from obvious criticism. The "traditions" of the Jews were considered just as binding upon the Jews as the provisions of the law itself. These traditions of the fathers were additions to the law and comments upon its meaning. Naturally such a zealot would have nothing to do with the apostles except to persecute them, and therefore could not possibly have obtained the gospel from them.

2. Paul's Conversion (1:15,16a)

a. (1:15) *"But when it was the good pleasure of God, who separated me, even from my mother's womb, and called me through his grace."* Paul sets forth the doctrine of election very clearly here. In the words, "But when God, who selected me, was pleased," Paul indicates that his election was not because of his good works, zeal or good character, but wholly according to the good pleasure of God, unconditioned by anything pertaining to Paul. Paul proceeds to make it perfectly clear that he himself was passive in the election of God for his life's work, since it was manifested when he was unborn. He acknowledges that it was God who "set me apart [i.e., "elected" or "selected"] from my mother's womb." Paul witnesses to the Galatians, "God ... . called (me) by his grace." Paul's temporal calling was, of course, at the time of his conversion on the Damascus road, though his election for the task was from all eternity. Paul's effectual calling to his life's work was by the grace of God, that is, the unmerited favor of God, not because of his good works. Before his birth Paul was already elected to do the work God had selected him to do, so his good works and character could not possibly be the cause of that selection. In God's own time, however, God called Paul to his life's work, through the grace of God alone.

b. **(1:16a)** *"to reveal his Son in me."* Lightfoot thinks that the "in me," really means "through me," and represents Paul as the instrument of the revelation of the gospel to others. But in that case it would be difficult to see why Paul did not use the preposition *dia,* "through," instead of *en,* "in." Meyer thinks that this refers to the subjective revelation by God of the Son of God within the mind of Paul. That is, it was revealed to the consciousness of Paul that Jesus was indeed the Son of God, though up to that Damascus experience he had rejected his deity. As Meyer says, "Paul was . . . set apart by God, subsequently *called* at Damascus, and afterward provided inwardly with the *revelation of the Son of God,* in order that he might be able outwardly to *preach,* etc." In the phrase, *"in order that I might preach him as glad tidings among the Gentiles,"* "in order that" indicates the purpose of his calling and the revelation in his heart of the Son of God. It was all in order that he might preach the gospel to the Gentiles.

3. Paul after Conversion (1:16b—2:21)

a. Shows Himself Not Dependent on Other Apostles (1:16b-24)

(1) **(1:16b)** *"Immediately I conferred not with flesh and blood."* That is, Paul did not seek the guidance, instruction or advice of other men regarding his revelation from God, but departed for Arabia. The turning point in Paul's life was the conversion experience on the way to Damascus. It was then that God gave him his revelation of the Son in his inner consciousness. The immediate result of that experience was that Paul left Damascus at once and went to Arabia, without conferring with other Christian leaders. But does not this contradict the account of what happened in the Book of Acts? There he is said to have conferred with Ananias after three days' blindness, have remained several days with the disciples in Damascus, and then spoken repeatedly in the synagogues about Jesus as the Son of God. It is difficult to fit this Arabian visit into the chronology of Paul's life as found in Acts, but it would seem most likely to have occurred during the "certain days" of Acts 9:19, and would thus precede his preaching in the Damascus synagogues. On the other hand it is difficult to fit the "three years" of Galatians 1:18 into the Acts account, if we say that

the preaching in the Damascus synagogues and expulsion from Damascus took place *after* the Arabian experience. Where was Paul during those three years if he was not in Damascus? We must confess that we are ignorant of the precise order of events here, but that in no way means that either Paul's or Luke's account is in error. Possibly Luke did not know about the Arabian experience or what happened during the three years Paul here mentions, though since he wrote under the supervision of Paul, that seems unlikely. On the whole it would seem that the three years were passed in Damascus after his Arabian experience and before his expulsion from the city. Possibly it is to be inserted in the time mentioned in Acts 9:33, "when many days were fulfilled." At any rate Paul's word is to be accepted and we must therefore say that he did not at once confer with the other disciples but went to Arabia for an indefinite period of time. There he doubtless thought much about the doctrines of the faith, and possibly had the experience of divine revelation mentioned in II Corinthians 12:1-5.

(2) **(1:17)** *"Neither went I up to Jerusalem."* The expression "going up" to Jerusalem was always used with reference to travelling to that city. *"To them who were apostles before me."* He did not visit or see the other apostles during this time so of course did not get his gospel from them. *"I went away to Arabia."* We do not know how long he stayed in Arabia, but possibly he was there for considerable time before returning to Damascus and preaching in the Damascus synagogues. At any rate he was thoroughly grounded in the faith when he began to preach the gospel publicly in Damascus, so there was no opportunity for him to have gotten his gospel from the other apostles.

(3) **(1:18)** *"Then, after three years."* The problem is to decide the point when the three years began. Did the three years begin from the time of Paul's conversion? Or did they begin after the visit to Arabia and the stay in Damascus subsequent to that visit to Arabia? It seems quite evident that the three years began with the conversion of Paul, for his whole argument is that he was preaching the gospel for three years before he even saw Peter. When Paul says, *"I went up to Jerusalem to see Peter"* he is evidently referring to the journey mentioned in the 9th chapter of Acts. At first sight it might seem that there is a slight discrepancy between the two accounts, for Acts says, "But Barnabas took him and brought him to the apostles," while here in Galatians Paul insists that he saw only Peter and

James the brother of the Lord. The apparent discrepancy is resolved if we remember that Peter was really the representative of the apostles, and that James was the head of the Jerusalem church and honored almost equally with the apostles, as being the brother of Jesus. Since Paul was there only fifteen days it is quite probable that the other apostles were out on preaching tours in the country, so there was no opportunity to meet them.

(4) **(1:19)** *"But other of the apostles I did not see."* As we have just said, Peter was the representative of all the apostles. It is probable that the others were not in Jerusalem during those fifteen days. *"Except James, the brother of the Lord."* James occupied a unique position among the disciples. Technically he was not actually an apostle, but his native ability, the fact that he was the brother of Jesus and the fact that the whole church looked up to him as an equal of the apostles, gave him almost apostolic status. Then the fact that Jesus had appeared to him individually (I Cor. 15:7) led the disciples to regard him as being especially chosen by the Lord, and therefore having almost apostolic rank.

(5) **(1:20)** *"I lie not."* Paul makes the solemn statement that his readers may know that he did not obtain his apostleship from men. During his fifteen days in Jerusalem Acts tells us that Paul preached in the temple and disputed with the Greek proselytes, so it was perfectly clear that his gospel was in harmony with the true gospel, and that there was no opportunity for him to be taught it by the other disciples.

(6) **(1:21)** *"Then I came into the regions of Syria and Cilicia."* The reason he left so suddenly was that his enemies were plotting against his life, so the disciples sent him away from the city. Tarsus in Cilicia was his native city so that was the place to which he would naturally return. The fact that he also went to Syria before going to Cilicia would seem to indicate that he went by land, doubtless stopping at Antioch on the way. Then follows an indefinite period of time before he started work in Antioch at the invitation of Barnabas (Acts 11:26). He preached the gospel in Antioch for a year before the famine visit to Jerusalem (Acts 11:30).

(7) **(1:22)** It was during the fifteen day visit to Jerusalem above mentioned that Paul received the revelation that he was to leave Jerusalem because the Jews there would not receive his witness, and that he was to be sent to the Gentiles (Acts 22:17-21). Paul in verse 22 tells us that he was unknown by

face to the churches of Judea, which adds plausibility to the belief that the other apostles were not in Jerusalem at the time.

(8) **(1:23)** *"Only they were hearing."* The news kept coming to the churches of Judea that Paul was preaching the same faith which he had before persecuted. *"The faith."* We find that here at the very start of the Christian church the word "faith" or "the faith" had become another name for the gospel message, thus offering additional proof that preaching the gospel of salvation through faith alone was not a later addition to the teaching of Christianity as many Modernists claim, but was *the* message of the gospel from its beginning.

(9) **(1:24)** *"And they glorified God in me."* Paul's humility is to be noticed. He says that the Christians glorified not him but God. "Let your light so shine that they may glorify your father who is in heaven." Paul never claimed the glory for himself but always returned it to God. Though the Christian brethren were afraid to join themselves to him at first, after Barnabas introduced him to Peter and James, they did not hold a grudge against him but glorified God in him.

b. Recognized in Conference with Other Disciples as Already Chosen by God to Be an Apostle (2:1-10)

(1) **(2:1)** *"Then, after fourteen years I went up again to Jerusalem."* Through the years there has been a great dispute as to whether this visit is the visit at the time of the Council of Jerusalem (Acts 15), or the famine visit of Acts 11:30. If it was the famine visit, then the argument made by some modernists that Paul was guilty of concealing the evidence in his argument with the Galatians would fall to the ground, and also their argument that Paul agreed to a compromise regarding the gospel at the time of the Jerusalem Council would also collapse. That compromise is alleged to have been that Paul agreed to teach a part of the ceremonial law as necessary for the converts to keep. On the other hand, if we say that this is the reference to the Jerusalem Council of Acts 15, then Paul has passed over the famine visit in silence, and we are compelled to deal with the problem of the decrees of that council. If this visit is the one at the time of the famine, mentioned in Acts 11:30, then an early date for the writing of Galatians is possible, and the South Galatian churches would seem to be the ones involved in the heresy refuted in the Epistle to the Galatians. The view that this is the famine visit certainly cannot be dismissed as an intellectual curiosity, and if the objections to the view that this

visit is the one at the time of the Jerusalem Council should prove unanswerable, then the other view might be accepted.

However the arguments in favor of the view that this visit is the one at the time of the Jerusalem Council are powerful, and the objections to it are not insuperable. To begin with, the persons mentioned are the same in both cases. Barnabas and Titus were both present at the Jerusalem Council. James, who is mentioned first in the list of the apostles in Galatians 2:9, seems to have been the head of the church in Jerusalem in Acts 15:13 ff. The subject discussed seems to have been the same in both instances, namely, whether circumcision and keeping the ceremonial law should be required of the Gentile converts. Now if that fundamental question regarding the keeping of the ceremonial law as a requirement for becoming a Christian had been actually settled at the time of the famine visit, there would seem to have been no reason for holding the Jerusalem Council at a later date. If it be replied that the question was one that would not down (as the activities of the Judaizers referred to in the Galatian epistle seem to indicate), then it would indeed be strange that no appeal was made to the decision of an earlier council at the time of the famine visit. At least a mention of the earlier decision would seem to have been inevitable.

Moreover the objections to identifying this visit with the visit at the time of the Jerusalem Council are not insuperable. First, what shall we say to the fact that if this is the visit mentioned in Acts 15, Paul has passed over the famine visit in silence? Well, the account of the famine visit in Acts 11:30 makes no mention of the presence of the apostles in Jerusalem at that time, so if Paul did not meet the apostles at all then, there would be no reason to mention that visit as far as his argument is concerned. The churches of Judea at that time were subjected to severe persecution, and it may well be that the apostles were in hiding away from Jerusalem. That fact may have been known to the Gentile churches, so that they would know that Paul had no contact with the apostles at the time of the famine visit. Herod's persecution probably drove the apostles away from Jerusalem into surrounding Judea.

But what about the decrees of the Jerusalem Council? Would Paul be compromising his principles to have agreed to those decrees? The answer is no. Not only did Paul agree to the decrees of the Council according to the Book of Acts, whether the council was before or after the time of the writing of Galatians, but he did agree willingly. The fact that he made no apparent attempt to oppose the decrees, is in itself a strong argument in support of the view that the decrees in no way constituted a compromise of his principles. The truth for which Paul was contending was that salvation is by faith in Christ *alone,* not by *doing* something, like being circumcised, in addition to faith in Christ. That principle was recognized, and it is not stated that the decrees of the council should be kept by the Gentiles to secure salvation. They were recommended to the Gentiles as matters of expediency because of the many Jews in the regions where there were Gentile churches.

The decree of the council was that the Gentiles should refrain from fornication, from the pollution of idols, from things strangled, and from blood. Refraining from those things was the expedient thing to do for Christians in such circumstances. Fornication and idolatry were sins which Christians could not commit as Christians. Paul had circumcised Timothy who was half Jew, to avoid the criticism of the Jews, not because he thought circumcision was in any way necessary for salvation. In the same way he was willing to have the Gentiles keep such things as mentioned in the decrees, *as long as they were not required in order to become a Christian!* Of course Christians under all circumstances should refrain from fornication and idolatry as part of the moral law, the Christian's rule of life. If we are Christians we will want to keep the law of God, but we must not think that even such conduct as refraining from fornication is in any way a means of salvation.

The Western text of the Book of Acts omits the words, "and things strangled." If this were the correct reading (which it probably is not) it would remove all difficulty with the decrees, for the word "blood" could then be interpreted as "murder." The other items would then be a reference to the moral law. But this explanation is unnecessary if what we have said above is true.

(2) **(2:2)** *"I went up according to revelation."* The question is, to whom was the revelation given and what was the revelation? Some commentators say that it refers to the whole church in Antioch. Others, who think that the visit was the famine visit, say that it refers to the revelation given to the prophet Agabus. This of course is impossible if the visit was the one at the time of the Jerusalem Council, as we believe it was. The most logical explanation is that the revelation refers to one received by Paul when the church wished to send Barnabas and

Paul to Jerusalem to have the question raised by the Judaizers settled. *"I laid before them."* Who were the people here mentioned? Were they the church in Jerusalem as a whole, or were they the apostles only? The phrase, "privately to those of repute," would seem to indicate the apostles were the ones to whom he revealed his gospel. But the phrase is capable of another interpretation. Paul may be saying, "I laid before them the gospel which I preach among the Gentiles, and privately to those of repute," that is, there were two conferences, one before the church at large and the other before the leaders of the church. This is supported by the evidence of the Book of Acts regarding the Jerusalem Council, in which the whole church participated. Though no private conference is mentioned in Acts, it is quite probable in view of the gravity of the issues involved. But why does he use the term *"to them of repute"?* He may be quoting the Judaizers, or, more probably, may simply be stating the reason for appealing to the apostles; that is, because, though he needed no confirmation of his gospel for himself, others were comparing it to that preached by the apostles, and claiming that it was different. "So," says Paul, "since you appeal to the men of repute, let us see what they said about my gospel." *"Lest somehow I should be running, or had run, in vain."* Paul does not mean that there was doubt in his own mind about the validity of his gospel. He means that the Judaizers were seriously interfering with his work, and if allowed to continue would make all his work in vain. It was necessary, therefore, to get the endorsement of the Jerusalem church, and particularly of the leaders to whom the Judaizers were appealing, in order to continue his preaching effectively.

(3) **(2:3)** *"Not even Titus, who was with me, though he was a Greek, was compelled to be circumcised."* What is the exact meaning here? Certainly it was not that the apostles wanted to compel Titus to be circumcised and Paul successfully prevented it, for in that case they would hardly have given Paul the right hand of fellowship (verse 9). Nor does it mean that Titus was not *compelled* to be circumcised, but did so voluntarily, for in that case there would have been no point in bringing up the case of Titus, since it would not support Paul's argument. The meaning would seem to be that the Judaizers sought to circumcise Titus but Paul and the apostles prevented it, so that Titus was not compelled to be circumcised.

(4) **(2:4)** *"But because of false brethren stealthily brought in."* This whole phrase has no predicate to complete the

thought, and is very difficult to interpret. There are three possible interpretations in harmony with the position taken above: (1) Paul begins a new sentence in verse 4, but breaks it off and does not finish the sentence because what he wanted to say is included in the clauses following; (2) Paul is defining more closely the compulsion which was resisted by Paul and the apostles; (3) Paul is connecting this clause with verses one and two and is saying something like this: "I went up to Jerusalem, it is true, and had a conference with the apostles, on account of the false brethren stealthily brought in, in order to silence their propaganda." Each of these explanations make sense, and agrees with the argument Paul is making, namely that he was in no way subservient to the other apostles and did not get his gospel from them. Why does he call the Judaizers "false brethren"? Probably because they pretended to be Christians, but were at heart Pharisees rather than Christians, for they were depending on their law-works for salvation, rather than on Christ alone. *"Who sneaked in to spy out the freedom which we have in Christ Jesus."* The false brethren sneaked into the church at Antioch in order to spy out the rumored freedom from the Mosaic Law which the Gentiles were reputed to enjoy. They pretended to be true Christians but were opposed to the very heart of Christianity, salvation by faith in Christ alone. The "liberty" or "freedom" which they came in to destroy was the freedom from the requirements of the Mosaic Law, which freedom Paul introduced among the Gentile converts. This same freedom from law is being attacked by Modernists today who talk about "the spirit of Jesus," meaning not at all the Holy Spirit, but an attitude of tolerance of false doctrine assumed to be characteristic of Jesus. Showing this "spirit of Jesus" in our life is really to trust in our "sweet reasonableness of character" as a means of salvation. Only faith in Christ alone can save us today as in Paul's day. That does not mean tolerance of sin.

(5) **(2:5)** *"To whom we did not yield in subjection for even an hour."* At the close of the preceding verse Paul has stated that the purpose of the false brethren was to bring the Gentile Christians under bondage to the Mosaic Law, particularly circumcision. Here he declares that he did not yield to their demands for a single moment. *"That the truth of the gospel might be preserved to you."* This sets forth the reason Paul was so insistent in his opposition to the Judaizers: to preserve the truth of the gospel for all, but especially for the Gentile Christians, of whom the Galatian Christians were the type. The

phrase, "to you," cannot be used as a decisive argument in support of the North Galatian theory, as indicating that they were not yet evangelized at the time of this council, though it must be confessed that there seems to be an aura of the future preaching of this gospel surrounding the phrase. Of course it might refer to those who were already Christians, and support the South Galatian theory.

(6) **(2:6)** *"But from those who were reputed to be something."* This phrase is what is called an "anacoluthon." That is, it is an uncompleted sentence. Paul intended to say, "I received nothing," as the conclusion of the sentence, but he starts the following parenthetical clause and never goes back to finish the sentence, for the following verses imply that he received nothing from the apostles. "Reputed to be something," in no way indicates disrespect for the apostles, but rather contrasts the Judaizers, who were really nothing, with the apostles who were, after all, apostles, and so were "something." He however hastens on to the next clause, *"what formerly they were makes no difference to me; God does not accept the countenance of a man."* The word *pote,* here translated "formerly," is usually translated with the preceding word, "whatsoever." If it here means "formerly," as we think it does, then the thought is, "Even though the apostles formerly were with Jesus for three years, that fact makes no difference to me now that I have direct apostleship from the Lord; God does not accept the countenance of a man." That is to say, God is not partial to men because they have a good reputation. *"For to me those of repute added nothing."* This is the whole point of Paul's argument. The reason it made no difference to Paul who or what the leaders of the church were, except for the fact that the Judaizers appealed to them against Paul, was that they added nothing to his gospel or to his commission. This was the important point for which he was contending. He had a supernatural calling to be an apostle, and the fact was established by the fact that the apostles recognized it as such. But why does Paul go to so much trouble to establish his independence of the other apostles? It certainly was not egotism on his part that led him to insist on this. Paul was, in effect, contending for Jesus Christ himself. Christ had given him his apostolic commission. He was empowered to write his epistles. In contending for his independence he was defending his gospel of salvation by faith alone which Christ had revealed to him.

(7) **(2:7)** *"But, contrariwise, when they saw that I was en-*

trusted with the gospel of the uncircumcision, even as Peter with the gospel of the circumcision." This does not imply that there was any difference in the gospel preached to the two classes of people. It was simply defining the spheres of their respective activity.

(8) (2:8) "*For he who wrought in Peter unto the apostleship of the circumcision worked also in me unto the Gentiles.*" God worked in Peter in preaching to the Jews and he worked in Paul in the same way to preach to the Gentiles. Though the apostles had different spheres of activity, it was God working through them that produced fruit.

(9) (2:9) "*And when they recognized the grace that had been given me.*" Here is the specific recognition of Paul's apostolic commission from God. In talking with Paul they soon discovered that he had a commission as an apostle from God himself, so they could not interfere nor could they add or subtract from his gospel message. "*James and Cephas and John.*" James, the brother of the Lord, had become the bishop of the church in Jerusalem, and as such is here put first in the list, though elsewhere Peter is put first because of his spokesmanship for the apostles at large. Probably the other apostles are not mentioned here because the three mentioned were actually the leaders. "*Those reputed to be pillars.*" It was customary for the Jews to speak of the great teachers af the law as "pillars." Paul does not mean to say that these apostles were not *really* pillars, but were only reputed to be pillars; he means that because the Judaizers considered them to be pillars, he would mention what they said about him in this connection. "*Gave to me and Barnabas the right hands of fellowship.*" The giving of the right hand was the symbol of alliance, and proved that the apostles approved of the gospel Paul and Barnabas were preaching. "*That we should go to the Gentiles and they to the circumcision.*" The other apostles recognized that Paul had received a special commission from Christ to preach to the Gentiles, so they agreed to carry out their separate fields of activity. This does not mean that Paul was *not* to preach to the Jews as opportunity arose, but rather that his special field of activity was as an apostle to the Gentiles.

(10) (2:10) "*Only that we should remember the poor.*" The tense of the verb "remember" indicates continued action. They asked Paul to keep on remembering the poor as he had been doing in the collection for the poor. "*Which very thing I was eager to do.*" We do not know the specific help that Paul gave

the poor of Jerusalem after the Jerusalem Council up to the time of the writing of this letter, but knowing the generous nature of Paul it is safe to assume that he collected alms for the saints at Jerusalem wherever he went, and forwarded it to them.

c. Shows by Rebuking Peter at Antioch That He Is Not Inferior to Peter or the Other Disciples (2:11-21)

(1) Peter's Hypocrisy at Antioch Caused Paul to Rebuke Him Publicly (2:11-14a)

(a) **(2:11)** *"But when Cephas came to Antioch I withstood him to the face."* In showing his independence from the disciples, Paul now shows that he rebuked Peter to his face before the church, so that he could not have been subservient to him. This probably took place soon after the Jerusalem Council, when Peter visited Antioch. *"Because he stood condemned."* Does this mean that the Christian community condemned Peter, or that Paul was convinced his action was worthy of condemnation? Probably the latter, though it is possible the community also condemned Peter's actions.

(b) **(2:12)** *"For before that certain came from James."* It is not necessary to hold that James actually sent them to make the Christians break off table fellowship. James was the head of the Jerusalem church, and this phrase may mean simply that these men were close friends of James. In view of the wise way he acted at the Council it is hard to believe he would support the activities of the Judaizers. *"He was eating with the Gentiles."* While the custom of eating separately from the Gentiles in order to avoid offense was not intrinsically wrong, it was wrong for him to *pretend* that he was living as a Jew when he had been living differently. *"But when they came he drew back and separated himself, being afraid of those who were of the circumcision."* "Those of the circumcision" were of course the same ones who had come from James. There was nothing wrong with his separating himself from the Gentiles if he wanted to do so, but it was wrong for him to act the part of a hypocrite regarding it. Why did Paul rebuke Peter publicly? Normally the thing for him to do would have been to approach Peter privately about the matter. Peter's action, however, was a public action, giving the impression that separation from the Gentiles in eating was necessary for salvation. It demanded a public rebuke for the sake of the whole church and the gospel itself.

(c) **(2:13)** *"And with him the rest of the Jews acted insincerely."* The terrible feature of the situation was that Peter's example led astray the rest of the Jewish Christians. Were this to go unchecked it might well mean that the whole church would begin to teach that the Jews, because they were circumcised, were a better class of Christians than the Gentiles. *"So that even Barnabas was carried away with their dissembling."* "Even Barnabas" carries with it the disappointment and heartbreak that Paul felt at the actions of the Jewish Christians in siding with the Judaizers, especially when Barnabas went along with them.

(d) **(2:14a)** *"But when I saw that they were not walking straight according to the truth of the gospel, I said to Cephas before them all."* The hypocrisy of Peter and Barnabas was that they were concealing their real principles in order to keep the peace and avoid offending the Judaizers. They were putting expediency above principles and truth. In rebuking Peter publicly Paul was running the risk of "splitting the church." Had Peter had less humility and spiritual sensitivity, he might have been indignant at Paul and "split the church." Paul, however, was one who put truth above consequences. Considering expediency was not wrong when no principle would be violated, but if the gospel would be compromised by keeping still, then loyalty to Christ demanded that he speak out even if it caused a split in the church. The "truth of the gospel" was the thing that made it necessary for Paul to take the action he did. The truth which he defended was that we are justified, not by rites and ceremonies, not by law keeping or good works, but through faith in Christ alone. It was unfair of Peter to try to make the Gentiles keep the law when he himself knew it was unnecessary to keep it in order to be saved.

(2) The Rebuke Was an Exposition of the Gospel Paul Preached (2:14b-21)

(a) **(2:14b)** *"If thou being a Jew livest as the Gentiles do and not as the Jews."* Some have held that the speech to Peter ended with the 14th verse, but the rest of the chapter follows so naturally that one cannot but conclude that it was part of the rebuke. What follows gives us the very heart of the gospel. The one problem in this passage is the meaning of "livest." Does the word refer to the high sense of eternal life and say, "If you are living having the gift of eternal life on the same conditions as the Gentiles have it, that is, through faith in Christ alone, why do you give the impression that salvation is received as a reward for keeping the Jewish law?" This is a true thought, but probably the word "livest" simply means ordinary mode of life, and Paul is saying, "If you are living without keeping the Mosaic Law ordinarily, why are you now giving the impression that living as a Jew is a higher kind of life, or that it is a life-mode necessary for salvation?" *"How is it that you are compelling the Gentiles to Judaize?"* In what sense did Peter "compel" the Gentiles to Judaize? It was the compulsion of an example. The more sincere the Gentile Christians were the more likely would they be to follow Peter's example and feel that they had to become Jewish proselytes if they wanted to become higher class Christians who associated on equal terms with the Jewish Christians. The verb "to Judaize" means to begin to observe the Mosaic ceremonial law, eventually even to become circumcised.

(b) (2:15) *"We are by nature Jews and not sinners of the Gentiles."* Calling the Gentiles "sinners" was simply to use the old Jewish division of mankind into Jews and "sinners."

(c) (2:16) *"But, knowing that a man is not justified by works of the law."* The word "to justify" does not mean "to make righteous" but "to declare righteous" regardless of the sinful condition of the individual. This is the distinction between Protestant and Roman Catholic Christianity. Protestants believe that we are justified or declared to be righteous in the sight of God through faith in Christ who was righteous in our place. Imparted or infused righteousness does not precede salvation as the Romanists declare, but follows salvation. Justifying a man is like a judge pronouncing a sentence of acquittal upon a prisoner in the court. *"But only through faith in Christ Jesus, even we believed in Christ Jesus."* The words which Paul used, *ean me,* literally mean "except" or "unless"; but such a meaning would contradict Paul's whole argument and make him say that man *can* be justified by works of the law if he is helped by faith in Christ. As Machen says, "That was almost exactly the view of Paul's opponents, the Judaizers. Certainly, therefore, Paul cannot mean to give expression to it here." What he is trying to say is that "a man is not justified at all except through faith in Christ Jesus." *"Even we believed in Christ Jesus, in order that we might be justified by faith in Christ and not by works of the law, because by the works of the law no flesh shall be justified."* Paul is recalling to Peter the fact that they both believed in Christ Jesus in order to be declared righteous by faith in Christ, not by works of the Mosaic law. These works are the kind Peter was doing when he withdrew himself from the Gentiles, as though they were not good enough to eat with! The last clause is quoted from Psalm 143:2, and the whole verse reiterates the doctrine of justification through faith in Christ alone.

(d) **(2:17)** *"But if in seeking to be justified in Christ, we ourselves also were found sinners, is Christ a minister [or agent] of sin?"* Machen's paraphrase of 2:17-19a is excellent: "We Jews, when we became Christians, gave up seeking justification through the law; we became just as much 'sinners' (in the old Jewish sense of the word, which divided humanity into two classes of (1) Jews and (2) sinners), as the Gentiles. But it was Christ who led us to take this step. If so, if Christ led us to become 'sinners,' how shall we avoid the conclusion that Christ was one who led us into sin? Only by recognizing that Jewish distinction between 'sinners' and Jews is invalid. We must not set it up again. If we do set it up again, then we do charge Christ with being a helper in sin. Christ led us to become 'sinners' in that Jewish sense of the word. If that sense is right, then, since Christ led us to become 'sinners,' He led us into sin." Paul, before explaining or answering the blasphemous question "Is Christ a minister of sin?" follows it at once with the phrase, *"God forbid!"* which literally means, "may it not be (so)." The answer comes in the following verses.

(e) **(2:18)** *"For if the things I tore down I again build up, I show myself to be a transgressor."* The connection "for" would seem to be not with the words "God forbid" but with the thought of the sentence, "Is Christ a minister of sin?" The things which they tore down were of course the seeking justification through keeping the Mosaic law, while the things they would be building up would be again seeking justification through keeping or trying to keep the Mosaic law. If we do that, says Paul, we are not making Christ a minister of sin, but are simply making ourselves transgressors. The transgression would be the obvious one of confessing that it was wrong to tear down the keeping of the Mosaic law.

(f) **(2:19)** *"For I through the law died to the law that I might live unto God."* The "for" at the beginning of this verse introduces a reason for verses 17 and 18. "As for me," says Paul, "I will not have anything to do with the idea of keeping the law as a means of salvation. Why should I confess that I am a transgressor in tearing down the law? Through the law I came under the curse of the law as a law-breaker, but because I have been crucified with Christ (verse 20) I have died to the law in the death of Christ. The purpose of that death to the law is in order that I might live unto God." The thought of this verse is paralleled in Romans chapter 7. In the person of Christ, with whose death we are identified, we have died to the law, and are therefore free from it and are now free to live unto God.

(g) (2:20) *"I have been crucified together with Christ."* The thought of this clause is connected with the preceding verse. Indeed it is sometimes included in verse 19. This is the union with Christ by faith which unites us with his death to sin (Romans chapter 6) as well as to his resurrected life to right-eous living. When Christ died, believers died, because he died in their place and bore death as their substitute. That had a definite purpose, however, namely, that they should live holy lives unto God, not as a means of salvation, but because they love God. *"And it is no longer I that live, but Christ liveth in me."* Here we have the union with Christ through faith; the identification of one's will with the will of Christ, so that we desire what Christ desires, and live the life of the new birth as Christ would have us live it. This does not mean loss of per-sonal identity in a pantheistic sense, but rather the union of a bride with her husband so that she wants to please him in everything. So we want to please Christ. *"And the life which I now live in the flesh, I live in the faith which is in the Son of God who loved me and gave himself for me."* "The life which I now live in the flesh." In saying that he has died to the law by his death with Christ's death, Paul is not saying on the one hand that he is merely dead to ceremonial law that he might keep the moral law. He is dead to *all* law as a means of earning one's salvation. But on the other hand Paul is not saying that Christians do not need to keep the law because they are not under law but under grace. The life which he now lives in the flesh is a life of faith in the Son of God. Living "in the faith" involves living a holy Christian life, for that is the life unto which we have been saved. Union with Christ by faith, so that Christ is living in us means that we hate the sin Christ hates and love the holy things Christ loves. In other words we are dead to the law as a means of salvation but alive to the law as a way of living. "Who loved me and gave himself for me." The substitutionary atonement of Christ is taught in these words. Living in the faith also means that we have to take our right-eousness on faith, for we are unrighteous. But Christ was our substitute, both in dying for us and in his life of obedience for us. He not only died in our place but kept the law in our place. We have to take that on faith, however, so our salvation is all, past, present and future, a life of faith in the Son of God who loved us and gave himself for us.

(h) (2:21) *"I do not make void the grace of God; for if righteousness is through the law, then Christ died in vain."* As Dr. J. Gresham Machen says, this verse is the key verse of the epistle to the Galatians. If, as the Judaizers were claiming, obedience to the law was partly necessary for salvation, then the work of Christ in his death was really in vain. As Dr .Benjamin Warfield used to say, if we must put one stitch in the garment of righteousness God has provided for us in Christ's righteousness, then no one will be saved, for all our righteousnesses are as filthy rags. No obedience can be perfect obedience so *all* our faith must rest in Christ for salvation, and not in ourselves. Trusting in law keeping would make void the grace of God in Christ.

II. *PAUL DEFENDS HIS GOSPEL* (3:1–4:31)

A. An Argument from Experience (3:1-5)

1. The Galatians Received the Spirit through Faith, Not Works of the Law (3:1-5)

a. (3:1) *"O foolish Galatians, who hath bewitched you?"* Paul does not tell us how Peter took the rebuke in the latter part of the second chapter, but since he says that his principles were the same as Peter's, and that it was Peter's inconsistency in applying those principles to which he objected, we may conclude that Peter took the rebuke in good grace. In the latter verses of the second chapter Paul had pictured the wonderful grace of God in Christ's righteousness received by faith alone, and now he can hardly contain himself, as he utters these words in 3:1. They must be out of their normal minds to depart from the gospel in such a way. *"Before whose eyes Jesus Christ was openly pictured as crucified."* Paul here gives us an example of his missionary preaching. He pictured the crucifixion of Christ to his hearers among the Gentiles. He tells us elsewhere (I Cor. 1:23) that he made the crucifixion of Christ the center of his missionary message. He tells the Corinthian Christians that he determined to preach this almost exclusively (I Cor. 2:2). That was what he did in Galatia, and now he recalls it to his readers. The doctrine of the atonement of Christ was the very center of Paul's preaching to unbelievers. The Textus Receptus includes the words, *"that you obey not the truth,"* after the words, "who hath bewitched you?" Most manuscripts omit them, but they make good sense, and quite possibly were a part of the original manuscript.

b. (3:2) *"This only I wish to learn from you: Was it by works of the law that ye received the Spirit, or was it by the hearing of faith?"* It would take only one thing to refute the Judaizers, namely, considering the way the Spirit was received, by faith not works. By "Spirit" Paul is referring especially to the "charismata," the special gifts of the Spirit which were bestowed on believers by the laying on of the hands of an apostle. That he has this in mind is seen by verse 5. If they received these gifts of the Spirit by faith, how foolish it is to think some higher gift can be received by law keeping! In using the term, "this only" Paul does not mean that this is his only argument on the point.

He means that he is using an argument from their own experience which alone should be sufficient to convince them of their
error in thinking law works would give salvation.

c. (3:3) *"Are ye so foolish? Having begun in the Spirit do ye
now make an end in the flesh?"* Making "an end in the flesh,"
means trusting in human merit rather than in Christ alone for
salvation. The "so" in the beginning of the verse refers to what
follows, not to the preceding verse. Probably the Galatians
thought they were going more deeply into the things of the
Spirit, while they were keeping law works, but this was self-
delusion.

d. (3:4) *"Have ye suffered so many things in vain? if indeed
it be in vain."* This is a reference to persecution suffered by
the Galatian church previous to this time. We have no record
of such persecutions, but at that time becoming a Christian
almost inevitably brought persecution. Paul can hardly believe
that all that was in vain. There is perhaps a hint that the Jews
instigated the persecution, in the words "in vain." Perhaps Paul
is saying, "If you had kept the law in the first place you would
not have been persecuted, so your sufferings were in vain if you
now go back to law keeping as a means of salvation."

e. (3:5) *"He therefore who supplieth to you the Spirit and
worketh miracles among you, doeth he it by works of the law
or by the hearing of faith?"* Here clearly, the reference to the
Spirit is to the supernatural powers bestowed by the Holy Spirit
on believers at that time. We are not to think that they are
necessary for all Christians. At that time they seem to have been
bestowed only in the presence of apostles. Cf. the disciples of
John in Acts 19:6.

B. The Argument from Scripture (3:6-22)

1. Abraham Was Justified by Faith, Not Works of the Law
(3:6)

(3:6) *"Even as Abraham believed God, and it was reckoned
to him for righteousness."* Here we have the doctrine of justification by faith alone specifically set forth. The answer to the
question ·in the preceding verse is taken for granted: "it was by
hearing of faith." Abraham believed God before his circumcision and four hundred and thirty years before the law was
given, so if he was saved at all it was by faith alone.

2. Believers Are True Children of Abraham (3:7)

(3:7) *"Know, therefore, that they that are of faith, these are
the children [sons] of Abraham."* The Judaizers had emphasized

the idea that only the blood descendants of Abraham were those who had a right to claim the promises God gave to Abraham. They reluctantly admitted that those who had by circumcision become Jews could also claim the promises given to Abraham. Paul, however, insists that those receiving the blessings promised to Abraham must have the faith of Abraham. They only are the true children of Abraham, whether Jews or Gentiles. The promises given to the descendants of Abraham are therefore to all Christians who have Abraham's faith, not merely to those who are Jews by nature. If this be true, then we must not look for future blessings to be bestowed on racial Jews who reject Christ as their Messiah.

3. Believers Are Therefore the True Heirs of the Promise to Abraham (3:8,9)

a. (3:8) *"And the Scripture, foreseeing."* Notice that Paul assumes that the Scripture written is in itself prophetic. He does not hold the idea that Scripture is only the Word of God when it "finds" a man, that is, that the words of Scripture are only important when they are used by God to impinge the revelation of God directly inside a man's soul. Paul holds that the words as written down in Scripture are themselves the Word of God, whether they "find" a man or not. *"That God would justify the Gentiles by faith."* The words "by faith" are emphasized by preceding the other words. Personifying Scripture, it is as though God were actually seen by the written Scriptures in the act of justifying the Gentiles by faith. *"Proclaimed the gospel beforehand to Abraham, saying, In thee all the nations shall be blessed."* The fact that *all* the Gentiles were to be blessed made it impossible to claim that *only* Jews could be heirs of the promises. "Preached the gospel to Abraham." The promises given to Abraham are the gospel, says Paul. The promise of a coming Messiah was implied in the phrase in question.

b. (3:9) *"So then those who are of faith are blessed with the believing Abraham."* In concluding the first part of Paul's argument from Scripture, the apostle categorically declares that anyone who has faith, that is, faith in Christ in this gospel age, is blessed together with the believing Abraham. The Gentiles, therefore, who have such faith are blessed apart from obedience to the Mosaic law. "Blessed with the believing Abraham" is equivalent to "are justified with the believing Abraham."

4. The Law Brought a Curse, Not a Blessing. Christ Re-

deemed Us from the Curse of the Law by Becoming a Curse
for Us (3:10-14)

a. (3:10) *"For as many as are of the works of the law are
under a curse."* The phrase, "as many as," indicates a group of
whom those in question have the quality asserted, in this case
being under a curse. The whole unbelieving world needs salvation because all are sinners, but of that group those who trust
in the works of the law for salvation are singled out as being
under a particular curse. The argument Paul is making is really
a continuation of the argument in the preceding verse. Those
who have faith like Abraham's faith are blessed. But those who
do not have such faith and trust in keeping the law are under
a curse. Obviously a step in his argument is omitted. He implies the truth that no one has ever kept the law, for if one
had kept the law perfectly he would not be under the curse in
question. *"For it is written, 'Cursed is everyone who does not
abide by all the things written in the book of the law to do
them.'"* The quotation is from Deuteronomy 27:26. But what
is the curse in question? It is of course the curse which was
stated in the passage in Deuteronomy 27. Paul is dealing with
the legalistic situation of those who, like the Judaizers, say that
the letter of the law must be obeyed in order to be saved. Paul
says, if those who trust in the works of the law for salvation are
right, then they are all under the curse from which there is no
human escape, for all have sinned.

b. (3:11) *"Now that in the law no one is justified with God
is clear, because 'the just shall live by faith.'"* The quotation
is from Habakkuk 2:4. If righteousness had been possible for
those who kept the law and trusted in it, there would have been
no reason for the other statement about righteousness being by
faith. There are just two possible ways of salvation: salvation as
a wage for what we do, and salvation as a free gift from God.
Since the fall no mere man has ever been able to keep the law
perfectly, so the "just shall live by faith." Receiving God's
righteousness in Christ as a free gift through trust in Christ for
salvation is the only possible way of becoming right with God.

c. (3:12) *"And the law is not of faith but 'he who has done
them shall live in them.'"* This quotation is from Leviticus 18:5.
We might conceivably be saved by either faith *or* works, but
not by both. The one who chooses to be saved by works is
bound to keep the whole law. His life must be lived in trust in
his good works. Since no one can keep the law perfectly it follows that no one can be saved by keeping the law. The law is

not faith, so we cannot trust in faith supplemented by good works. We are shut up to the way of faith in Christ if we are to receive eternal life.

d. (3:13) *"Christ redeemed us from the curse of the law by becoming a curse for us, because it is written, 'Cursed is everyone that hangeth upon a tree.'"* The law, then, brought a curse upon everyone, for no one has kept it. That curse had to be dealt with. Christ dealt with the curse by becoming a curse for us, in our place. The quotation is from Deuteronomy 21:23. Since Christ hung on a tree, he must have been cursed, not for his own sins because he had none, so it must have been in our place that he bore the curse. But who are the ones referred to in "Christ redeemed us"? Strictly speaking it would seem to refer primarily to the Jews, for only they were under the Mosaic curse. But that does not mean that Gentiles are not under a curse. Since they have the law of God written in their hearts (Romans 2:14 f.), when they do not keep it (and none has), they are under God's wrath (Romans 1:18) and need to be redeemed. Paul declares therefore that the blessing comes to the Gentiles, in the following verse.

e. (3:14) *"In order that unto the Gentiles the blessing of Abraham might come in Christ Jesus, in order that we might receive the promise of the Spirit through faith."* The word "redeemed" means to "buy back," or "to set free by the payment of a price." The price by which Christ redeemed us was his own blood shed on Calvary. That redemption was in order that the blessing promised to Abraham might come to us Gentiles. Are the two clauses introduced by "in order that" coordinate or is the second clause dependent on the first? Probably the latter for the receipt of the promise of the Spirit through faith comes as a result of the blessing in Christ Jesus, or perhaps as a part of that blessing. What is this "promise of the Spirit"? If it comes *after* the blessing in Christ Jesus, it can hardly be regeneration, for regeneration is that work of the Spirit which enables us to believe in Christ. In view of the other teaching of Paul (I Corinthians 12:1-11) this would seem to refer to the spiritual gifts bestowed by the laying on of the hands of the apostles (Acts 19:6), or to the "fruit of the Spirit" described in Galatians 5:22-23. Of course, if the second clause refers to regeneration, it would have to be co-ordinate with the first, for regeneration does not follow the blessings of Abraham in Christ Jesus, but is the first of those blessings, followed by the gift of faith in Christ. However, the "promise of the Spirit" seems to be a stereotyped phrase referring to the gifts which the Spirit gives believers. In that case, the clause would depend on the first.

5. The Law Came Later Than the Promise and Cannot Affect It (3:15-18)

a. (3:15) *"Brethren, I speak after the manner of men, even a confirmed covenant [will] of man no one sets aside or adds thereto."* Paul is softening his approach to the Galatians with the kind word, "brethren." Cf. 3:1. He is going to give an example from everyday life to prove his point that the later scribes and rabbis of the Jewish nation could not rightfully alter the terms of the covenant promises God gave to Abraham which were that righteousness was reckoned to Abraham through faith, not works. An ordinary contract or will when it has been officially made and accepted by both parties cannot be altered or added to by anyone. How much the more was it impossible for the Jewish religionists to alter the terms of God's promises to Abraham.

b. (3:16) *"But to Abraham and to his seed were the promises spoken. He does not say, 'And to seeds,' as of many, but as of one, 'And to thy seed,' which is Christ."* At first sight one might say that Paul here is quibbling over an unimportant point: whether the number of the noun is plural or singular. In English the argument would rest on the absence of one letter in the noun: *seed,* not *seeds.* In Greek the argument is over the addition of one letter and the changing of another. For Paul this is not only important, but the crux of his argument, showing incidentally his belief in the literal accuracy of the Bible text. His argument is that the use of the plural, *seeds,* would make the promises to the physical descendants of Abraham, while the use of the singular noun, *seed,* points to one descendant, Christ, and by inference to his church which is the body of Christ. If the word had been *seeds,* then the argument of the Judaizers might have a point, but the use of the singular noun, *seed,* ruled out the application of the promises to the literal physical descendants of Abraham alone. Since the word *seed* referred to Christ, the spiritual children of Abraham were included in Christ, as heirs of the promises. Now of course the original writer probably used the word thinking that it referred to the physical descendants of Abraham, and it is said that the plural of the word refers to grain, etc., so that the writer would not use it with reference to people. The fact remains, however, that the Holy Spirit so guided the writer of the Old Testament

passage in question that he used an expression which must refer
to Christ (and his mystical body, the church). It would be impossible to conceive of a higher doctrine of inspiration of the
Bible than that held by Paul in this passage.

   c. (3:17) *"Now this I say, a covenant confirmed beforehand
by God, to Christ, cannot be annulled by the law which came
four hundred and thirty years later, so as to make the promise
of no effect."* In Genesis 15:13 the length of the stay in Egypt
is given as four hundred years, obviously a round number. In
Exodus 12:40 it is given exactly as 430 years. Possibly the date
when the sojourn began is different in both cases. The covenant
promise cannot be rendered void by the law which came 430
years later. The promise given to Abraham was unconditional,
so it cannot be changed or made void by the law which was
given later.

   d. (3:18) *"For if the inheritance is of the law, it is no longer
by promise, but God granted it to Abraham through a promise."*
The working of the law and the promise are mutually exclusive.
If "the possession of the Messianic salvation proceeds from the
law, which must have been the case if God's covenant with
Abraham had lost its validity by means of the law, then this
possession comes no longer from promise, — a case which, al-
though necessary on that supposition, cannot occur, as is evident
from the precedent of Abraham, to whom salvation was given
by God through promise" (Meyer). The inheritance of the
promise is not through law. The inheritance mentioned is the
inheritance of all the Messianic blessings. The promise of this
inheritance was given by God to Abraham without any conditions except faith in God and his promises.

   6. A Purpose of the Law Was to Bring Knowledge of Sin
(3:19-22)
   a. (3:19) *"What then is the law? It was added for the sake of
transgressions, till the seed come to whom the promise hath
been made; (and it was) ordained through angels by [lit. 'in'] a
mediator's hand."* If salvation cannot be earned by keeping the
law, what is its purpose anyway? There is a real question as to
whether the phrase which in the original reads *ton parabaseon
charin* is to be translated "to check transgressions," or "to make
transgressions." *Charin* can mean either "for the sake of" or
"because of." Probably Paul intended to say that the law was
given to increase transgressions (cf. Rom. 5:20) so that men
would understand their helplessness and turn to Christ when

salvation by faith was understood. "The seed" refers to Christ. The phrase "ordained through angels" refers to Deut. 33:2, and means "administered by the medium of angels." The "mediator" is of course Moses. There is a contrast in Paul's thinking between the indirectness in the giving of the law and the directness of Christ's salvation to be received by faith alone of the believer.

b. (3:20) *"A mediator is not a mediator of one [person], but God is one."* Lightfoot says that there are between 250 and 300 different interpretations of this short verse. Probably the meaning is that the very idea of mediation implies two parties, while the promises given to Abraham were unconditional with God as the only party giving them. In this promise by God there were not two contracting parties. Jesus said that he and the Father were one, so God is one in that sense as well as the one party to the promise. The Promise was simply *given* by God.

c. (3:21) *"Is the law then against the promises of God? May it not be so, for if a law had been given which could make alive, verily righteousness would have been by law."* The thought of the first question is, "Is there antagonism between the law and the promises of God?" If salvation cannot be obtained by the law, is there opposition to the law involved in the promise? Paul's reply is, "Of course not!" If there were competition between the law and the promises, God would be contradicting himself, but the law can give neither spiritual life or righteousness with God, for it is only the rule by which to live. The last clause sets forth Paul's teaching that if spiritual life exists, then it will be followed by faith and faith followed by justification, God-given righteousness imputed to the believer. If the law could impart life (which it cannot do) justification would have followed.

d. (3:22) *"But the Scripture shut up all things under sin."* Scripture is personified here, and used in place of God, showing Paul's view that when Scripture speaks, God speaks. "Shut up" means placed under condemnation as in a prison. "All things" is a neuter word while in a similar passage in Rom. 11:32, the masculine gender is used. Here the "all things" deals with mankind as a unit. All mankind are sinners. *"That the promise by faith in Jesus Christ might be given to them that believe."* This is a purpose clause showing the reason why Scripture shuts all men under sin. That reason was that the promise to Abraham might be by faith in Christ to all believers. The Galatians of course believed that faith in Christ was necessary to salvation, but they doubted whether faith alone was all that was necessary. Therefore here there is a double use of faith to emphasize the fact that faith apart from works was the only way of salvation.

C. Contrast between Life under the Law and Their Present Freedom (3:23—4:11)

1. Life under the Law Was Like Being under a Tutor Who Was to Bring Them to Christ (3:23-25)

a. (3:23) *"But before faith came."* What is the time when "faith came"? Was it in the time of Abraham? But that cannot be the time, for the law had not been given at that time. Moreover, to whom did faith come? to Paul? to the Galatians? or to those who first trusted in Christ? or does this faith reach back to Old Testament times? It is difficult to decide, but it seems probable that Paul is referring to the period following the resurrection of Christ, and referring to the first Christians. *"We were kept in prison under the law shut up unto the faith to be revealed."* Paul here personifies the law as the jailor who kept all the Jews under the bondage of the law before faith in Christ was possible. The faith in Christ was a New Testament manifestation that made plain the fact that they no longer needed to try to keep the law to earn salvation.

b. (3:24) *"So that the law has been our tutor unto Christ, that we might be justified by faith."* The law is here pictured as a slave tutor or schoolmaster who conducted us to Christ, in order that we might be justified by faith. The law by setting up a standard of conduct impossible to attain, showed the Jews that salvation by law keeping was impossible, and all the time pointed to Christ who was to come in the future. This was for the purpose of making possible justification by faith.

c. (3:25) *"But faith having come we are no longer under the tutor."* Here the figure of the slave tutor, who went about with the boys to protect their persons and morals, is carried over to the period after the coming of Christ, and it is compared to the child coming of age when he is set free from the slave tutor. So the coming of the age of faith in Christ set the believers free from keeping the law as a means of earning salvation.

2. All Believers Are Now Children of God, Heirs According to the Promise (3:26-29)

a. All Believers Are United to Christ; Therefore They Are One in Him (3:26-28)

(1) (3:26) *"For ye are all sons of God, through faith in Christ*

Jesus." This is not a universal sonship of God, for all who are sons of God are such through faith in Christ Jesus alone. They are not naturally sons of God, but become such when they are adopted into God's family of believers at the time of their believing in Christ as Saviour.

(2) **(3:27)** *"For as many of you as were baptized into Christ did put on Christ."* The phrase, "as many as," indicates that there were two kinds of people baptized. Some were baptized *into* Christ, that is, they were united to him by faith, while others who were baptized with water were not true believers and so were not baptized *into* Christ by the mystical union with him. Now if one was baptized *into* Christ, he put on Christ as a garment, that is, he began to act as Christ would have him act. This is the thought of Romans 6:3 and Gal. 2:20.

(3) **(3:28)** *"There can be neither Jew nor Greek, there can be neither bond nor free, there can be no male nor [and] female; for ye are all one in Christ Jesus."* Here we have the true unity of believers. All believers of whatever race or station in life are one body in Christ Jesus. They are the true invisible church of God. They are all united in Christ. This is the equality of the kingdom of God. If then there was this unity among believers, how silly it was for the Judaizers to suggest that uncircumcised Christians were not as good as circumcised Christians. The previous divisions of race and religion were all blotted out in the unity of the faith in Christ. Here also we have the equality of women in Christ. Before Christ God does not put men on a higher plane than women.

b. All Believers Are Children of Abraham, Heirs of the Abrahamic Promises (3:29)

(3:29) *"And if ye are Christ's, then are ye Abraham's seed, heirs according to the promise."* Every true child of God, believing in Christ, belongs to Christ and therefore is a spiritual descendant of Abraham because he has the faith of Abraham. If he is a child of Abraham then he is an heir to all the promises given to Abraham. We are not to look forward to a time when the Jews will have special privileges in some future kingdom of Christ, for all those Old Testament promises were to the spiritual children of Abraham, and Gentile Christians are just as much heirs of those promises as Jewish Christians, and that too without circumcision.

3. Contrast between the Two Stages in the Life of Any Son (4:1-7)

a. A Child Is Like a Bondservant. So We Were Slaves to the Rudiments of the World before the Time of Christ (4:1-3)

(1) **(4:1)** *"But I say that so long as the heir is a child, he is no different from a slave, though he is lord of all."* The chapter begins with a further use of the illustration of the pedagogue-slave and a child. The comparison is between a child whose father is dead, but who is unable to assume control of his inherited property because of his childhood, and the world before the coming of the gospel. Both Jews and Gentiles were under the tutelage of the law at that time. Just as an heir is treated as a servant during his childhood, so before the gospel time all were under law.

(2) **(4:2)** *"But he is under guardians and stewards until the time appointed beforehand by his father [of the father]."* The use of the terms "guardians and stewards" indicates that it is a case of a child being orphaned but unable to control his inherited property until the time fixed in the father's will. Of course the comparison breaks down when we consider the father, for Paul does not mean to teach that God is dead. The only point he is making is that the heir is like a slave before he enters into his inheritance. Paul is subtly implying that those who are not under the gospel are still like infants when they subject themselves to the requirements of the ceremonial law.

(3) **(4:3)** *"So also we, when we were children, were enslaved under the rudiments [elements] of the world."* This would seem to be argument by ridicule, since Paul is asserting that those under the law are infants. The real problem in this verse is as to the meaning of "rudiments of the world." The primary meaning of the word in the original, *stoicheia,* refers to the letters of the alphabet. From that primary meaning the word denotes (1) the elements of the world such as fire, water, etc., and (2) "the alphabet of learning, rudimentary instruction." Augustine supposes that Paul is referring to worship of the physical elements by the Gentiles, but this meaning is excluded by the use of the word "we." Paul would seem to be dwelling on the rudimentary character of the law during the time when people were largely ignorant of the deeper spiritual truths. The "rudiments" then refer to elementary spiritual truths.

b. Now that Christ Has Redeemed Us from Being under the Law, We Are Like Children Who Have Come of Age and Are Free. As Sons We Are Heirs through God (4:4-7)

(1) **(4:4)** *"But when the fulness of the time came, God sent*

forth his Son, born of woman, made subject to law [born under the law]." "The fulness of the time came." This has a two-fold aspect. From God's point of view it was the predestined time for the coming of Christ. From the human point of view, it was the period in the development of history when the world was prepared for the gospel. The educational work of the law to show men the impossibility of earning salvation by works because of their sins was completed when Christ came. The expression "sent forth," teaches the pre-existence of the Son of God. "Born of a woman," primarily refers to the human nature of Christ, but is there not a hint that Paul knew of the virgin birth of Christ? "Born under the law," refers primarily to the Mosaic Law, but it includes all moral law, for Christ kept the law perfectly for us. The primary meaning of the word Paul here uses, *genomenon,* is "being made," though "born" would seem to be the best translation here.

(2) **(4:5)** *"That he might redeem them that were under the law, that we might receive the adoption (of sons)."* Here the purpose of his being made under the law is explained: it was to redeem those under the law by keeping the law in their place. The second *hina* clause is also a clause of purpose, and depends on the previous clause. He redeemed us so that we might become sons of God. The "law" here is primarily the Mosaic Law, but includes all law. Even Gentiles have the law of their conscience (Rom. 2:15). Being adopted into the family of God is the ultimate purpose of redemption, the climax of salvation.

(3) **(4:6)** *"And because ye are sons, God sent forth the Spirit of his Son into your hearts, crying, Abba, Father."* This is an experience which his readers all had of the witness of the Holy Spirit in the souls of Christians to their sonship of God, so that they utter instinctively the intimate cry of a babe to its father, Abba, Father! *Abba* is the Hebrew word for *papa,* the intimate love word for *father.* God here is said to send the Spirit, and the Spirit is "of the Son." Here we have the Trinity in one verse. The Spirit is the author of the intimate cry "Abba" that arises from the Christian experience of every Christian.

(4) **(4:7)** *"So that you are no longer a slave but a son."* This first clause returns to the metaphor of the son and the bond-slave, used in the previous verses. In our new relationship of sonship to God by adoption we have all the blessings of heir-ship, and Paul is calling all this to the attention of the Galatians that they may claim their privileges of sonship and reject the condition of slavery to which the Judaizers would seek to make

them return. The phrase *"and if a son, also an heir of God through Christ"* recalls to the readers their high calling in Christ Jesus. Heirship has countless privileges that the slave does not have. Why then return to slavery to the law? It is through Christ alone that we are heirs of God and have all the privileges of heirship.

4. The Christian Gentiles Were in Bondage to Idols, but Now Are Free (4:8-11)

a. **(4:8)** *"But at that time, not knowing God."* What was the time referred to? It was the time before they became Christians. Paul is now addressing the Gentile Christians in the Galatian church directly. *"Ye were slaves to those things which were by nature not gods."* That is, before they became Christians the Galatians worshipped idols. Paul uses this circumlocution out of tact, by pointing out the fact that what they previously worshipped were not naturally gods. Compare Isaiah 44:9-17.

b. **(4:9)** *"But now, having known God, or rather, having been known by God, how do ye turn back again to the weak and beggarly elements to which ye desire to be in bondage over again?"* The Greek word *gnontes,* here used, usually means experiential knowledge. "Having been known by God" puts the matter in the proper relationship. God is the one who initiates the knowing process as a result of regeneration. The "how turn ye again" is a remonstrance showing the revulsion of feeling Paul experiences at the very thought of the Galatians' apostasy. "The weak and beggarly elements" may refer to the rites and ceremonies of the Mosaic Law which were impossible to make one righteous, or it may refer to the elemental spirits of the world worshipped by the heathen (cf. 4:3). There were rites and ceremonies in the heathen worship as well as in the Mosaic Law, so Paul may be referring to both. Their desire to be again in bondage refers of course to these rites and ceremonies, such as are mentioned in the following verse.

c. **(4:10)** *"Ye observe days and months, and seasons and years."* This refers to the feasts and fasts common among the Jews. Apparently the Galatians had begun to observe these special feasts of the Jews and Paul is afraid that they will go the whole way and observe circumcision. The "years" may refer to the sabbatical years. Is the church today in the same danger of regarding special observance on special days as meritorious works?

d. **(4:11)** *"I am afraid of you, lest somehow I have labored* *over you in vain."* Paul was afraid of spiritual disappointment over a possible apostasy of the Galatians, but there is a deeper fear lest they should show by such apostasy that they are not really born again, so that all his preaching and trouble over them was in vain. Paul shows by the indicative mood that he is afraid this has already happened.

D. An Appeal to Be Loyal to the Gospel Because of Their Love for Him (4:12-20)

1. When Paul First Preached to Them They Received Him as an Angel of God in Spite of His Infirmity of the Flesh (4:12-15)

a. **(4:12)** *"I beseech you, brethren, become as I; for I also am as ye."* Does this mean (1) that Paul was once in bondage such as they are, or (2) that Paul has renounced his Jewish privileges and treated the Gentiles as brethren? Probably the latter as simpler grammatically, and more in accord with his intense feeling. To become as Paul was meant to trust only in the God-given righteousness obtained by trusting Jesus only.

b. **(4:13)** *"Ye did me no wrong; but ye know that because of the infirmity of the flesh I preached the gospel to you the first time."* Most texts and commentators include the first clause in the preceding verse. However the clause begins a new sentence and seems connected in thought with what follows, rather than the preceding sentence. The idea seems to be that he does not want them to think he is offended by what they have done recently or when he first was with them. "The infirmity of the flesh," refers to the sickness he had while with them the first time, which resulted in his staying with them to preach the gospel longer than he had probably intended. We do not know what that sickness was, though some believe it was some form of eye trouble or perhaps epilepsy. Paul is afraid they will not heed his pleas if they think they are caused by resentment on the part of Paul over previous ill-treatment, real or imaginary. Does "the first time" mean that Paul was there a second time? Quite probably it does, and thus refers to a visit paid during the third missionary journey.

c. **(4:14)** *"And that which was a temptation to me in my flesh."* This temptation in Paul's flesh seems to have been some repulsive sickness that might have caused the Galatians to look upon him with contempt. *"You did not despise nor look upon in contempt."* Whatever disfigurement or repulsive sickness Paul had, it did not cause the Galatians to turn from him at that time. *"But you received me as an angel of God, even as*

Christ Jesus." The Galatians were so delighted with Paul's message of salvation through Christ alone that they paid no attention to the infirmity in Paul's flesh. Had he been Christ himself or an angel from heaven they could hardly have listened to him with more joy. This makes their turning away to follow the Judaizers all the more astonishing.

d. (4:15) *"What has become of your joyousness? For I bear you witness that if possible you would have plucked out your own eyes and given them to me."* This text in the Textus Receptus reads somewhat different from that in the neutral text. The meaning in either case would seem to be somewhat similar, as translated above. "I bear you witness that if possible." This is a condition contrary to fact. It was not possible for them to do what follows. The clause which follows, "having plucked out your eyes you would have given them to me," is of course hyperbole, or exaggeration for effect. The clause shows how earnestly the Galatians originally loved Paul and wanted to do what he wanted them to do. This is one of the reasons many commentators think that the infirmity which Paul had was some sort of eye trouble.

2. Is Paul Now Their Enemy Because He Tells Them the Truth? (4:16)

(4:16) *"So then have I become your enemy because I tell you the truth?"* This may be either a question or a statement, but he would hardly declare himself to be their enemy, so it would seem to be a question. When he first preached to them he told them the truth but they did not regard him as an enemy for so doing. Why can they possibly think that he is opposed to them when he tells them the truth about the law and their relation to it?

3. Their Enemies Are Seeking Them to Shut Them Out of the Gospel (4:17,18)

a. (4:17) *"They seek you zealously for no good purpose; on the contrary they desire to exclude you [from the gospel] so that you will zealously seek them."* The purpose the Judaizers have in mind is to get the Galatians into a frame of mind in which they will doubt their salvation and then come to the Judaizers to learn law keeping. This is no figment of the imagination. That seems to have been actually happening in Galatia. Since the Gentiles knew very little of the Jewish law, if they began to doubt their own salvation they would naturally turn to the experts in the Jewish law and the prestige of the Judaizers would be enhanced.

b. **(4:18)** *"But it is good to be courted for a good purpose at all times, and not only when I am with you."* Paul is saying that it is all right to receive admiration if there is no sinister purpose in the minds of those who are doing the courting. It is a different matter, however, when flattery is offered insincerely for the purpose of getting the recipients to do what is wrong. The last clause would seem to recall their admiration for each other when Paul was with them. Paul enjoyed their love then and they enjoyed Paul's praise for their sincere Christianity. If others give such admiration to the Galatians that is all right with Paul unless it leads them to depart from the gospel teaching as the blandishments of the Judaizers were attempting to do.

4. Paul Pleads with Them as His Children (4:19,20)

a. **(4:19)** *"My little children, of whom I am again in birth pangs until Christ be formed in you."* The "of whom" is literally "whom," the accusative case, so that literally it is, "whom I again travail." Paul bursts out into a tender pleading with them to heed his appeal to reject the teaching of the Judaizers. "Again" refers to the first time when he was with them seeking to bring them to the new birth. Now he is forced again to go through the agony of trying to bring them into true life with Christ being formed in them. This is a figure of speech, but it is really true that a Christian is transformed into the image of Christ after his new birth. That is what Paul desires, for then he knows that there will be no permanent defection from the truth if Christ is truly formed in them.

b. **(4:20)** *"I could wish to be present with you this very hour and to change my voice, for I am perplexed about you."* Paul realizes that the words he has written may antagonize his readers in Galatia, so he says he could wish to be there with them if that were possible, so he could change the tone of his voice and let them know that his rebukes are given in love. He is perplexed as to how to write to them convincingly and also as to whether they will heed his word.

E. An Argument from the Allegory of Sarah and Hagar (4:21-31)

1. **(4:21)** *"Tell me, ye that desire to be under the law, do ye not hear the law?"* Even the law itself in telling the story of Ishmael and Isaac in Genesis, when rightly interpreted as Paul is about to do, supports his argument that only the children of

the promise are the spiritual children of Abraham, for the covenant promises were to Isaac and his seed, and withheld from Ishmael and his seed.

2. (4:22) *"For it is written that Abraham had two sons, one from the maid-servant, and one from the free woman."* The maid-servant was Hagar, the slave. While Paul's attention is focused exclusively on Ishmael and Isaac for the purposes of his allegory, that does not mean that he was ignorant of the other sons of Abraham by Keturah.

3. (4:23) *"But the son of the maid-servant was born according to the flesh, and the son of the free woman through the promise."* While both were Abraham's sons, there was a definite distinction in the way in which they were born. Abraham did not consult God when Sarah gave her bondslave to him as his wife, so Ishmael was born according to fleshly plans. Isaac, on the other hand, was definitely promised by God as the child of the covenant.

4. (4:24) *"Which things are an allegory; for these are the two covenants. The one from Mount Sinai, bearing children unto bondage, which is Hagar."* Paul does not mean that the literal history never occurred, but that there was a further symbolic sense than the literal facts. An allegory does not always mean an untrue story having a spiritual meaning. A true story can have, as in this case, a symbolic or allegorical meaning. This does not mean that we are free to give allegorical meanings to persons or events mentioned in Scripture unless Scripture itself does so. Some events were prophetical, for example, Jonah's experience which was prophetical of Christ's burial and resurrection. "Two covenants" refers to the fact that since Abraham had two wives, and a son by each wife, there was to be not one covenant, but two. The one covenant from Sinai represents the law, and just as Hagar was in bondage and her son Ishmael was therefore a child born in bondage, so the children of the law are figuratively in bondage to the law. The child of Sarah, Isaac, was the child of the promise, and was the child of the free-woman, so that those who are spiritual children of Abraham are free from the bondage of the law.

5. (4:25) *"Now Hagar is Mount Sinai in Arabia; and corresponds to the present Jerusalem, and she is in bondage with her children."* The point of the analogy is here definitely stated: Hagar corresponds to Mount Sinai in Arabia, and further corresponds to the earthly city of Jerusalem and the Jews. Just

as Hagar was in bondage, so the Jews were in bondage to the law.

6. (4:26) *"But the Jerusalem which is above is free, and she is our mother."* The other half of the comparison is between the heavenly Jerusalem with its children, that is, those who put their whole trust in Christ alone, and the Jews who trust in keeping the law. Those who trust in Christ are children of the heavenly Jerusalem and are free.

7. (4:27) *"For it has been written, Rejoice, thou barren that bearest not, break forth and cry, thou that travailest not; because the children of the desolate are more than of her that has her husband."* This is a quotation from Isaiah 54:1. "In the prophet's view, the 'woman which had her husband' was the visible Israel, possessing the temple and the other tokens of the Lord's dwelling in her midst; the 'desolate one' was the spiritual or the ideal Israel to be manifested in the future; for the present out of sight and seemingly in abeyance; but thereafter to be quickened into fertility by the inhabitation of the Lord" (Pulpit Commentary).

8. (4:28) *"But we, brethren, as Isaac was, are children of promise."* The neutral text has "ye are" in place of "we are," the reading of the Textus Receptus. We, like Isaac, are promised by God in his grace to receive salvation. The birth of Isaac was contrary to natural law. So we who are born again are born "not of bloods, nor of the will of the flesh, nor of the will of man, but of God" (John 1:13). There is one difference, however. In the case of Isaac it was the faith of the parents that made the promise effective. We, however, by believing ourselves through the quickening of the Spirit, enter into the promised salvation. But what is the meaning of "children of promise"? It might mean (a) children promised by God, or (b) children who have God's promise, or (c) children of God by virtue of the promise. The last interpretation is probably correct, for it was God's promise to save those who come to him through Christ that accounts for our being adopted children of God.

9. (4:29) *"But as then he who was born after the flesh persecuted him who was born according to the Spirit, so also now."* In this verse the real point of his allegory is brought to a focus. In Genesis 21:9, Ishmael mocked and ridiculed Isaac to such an extent that Sarah demanded that he be cast out of the home. So now the unbelieving Jews persecuted Jesus and his followers.

True Christians can always expect opposition and at times persecution from those who refuse to accept Christ as Saviour.

10. (4:30) *"But what saith the Scripture? Cast out the maidservant and her son: for the son of the maidservant shall not inherit with the son of the freewoman."* Cf. Gen. 21:10-12. The comparison between the driving away of Hagar and Ishmael from the covenant blessings in the home of Abraham, and the exclusion from salvation of those who reject Jesus Christ as Saviour is thus pointedly made by Paul. It was the sovereign act of God that separated Ishmael from the covenant blessings, and in like manner it is the sovereign choice of God that chooses men to salvation. There is therefore no place in the Christian church for legalism, since legalism has been condemned by God, just as Christ-rejecting Judaism was rejected by God in the time of Paul.

11. (4:31) *"So then brethren we are not children of the maidservant but of the free woman."* The neutral text has *dio,* "wherefore," in place of *ara,* "so then." The meaning is very similar, since a conclusion is being drawn from the preceding allegory. That conclusion is that Christians are alone the true children of Abraham and therefore of God. Numerous as were the Jews of that time, they were "children of the flesh," and therefore not the true Israel. This makes the legalism of the Judaizers to be clearly seen for what it was: a remnant of the fleshly Israel, having no part in the Christian church.

III. *THE CHRISTIAN LIFE IS ONE OF LIBERTY* (5:1–6:10)

A. An Appeal to Remain Free from the Yoke of the Law (5:1-12)

1. An Appeal to Stand Fast in Liberty (5:1)

(5:1) *"Stand fast, therefore, in the freedom wherewith Christ made us free; and be not again held in a yoke of bondage."* The translation of the American Revised Version, and the Revised Standard Version, "For freedom (did) Christ has set us free (Christ set us free), stand fast, therefore," has an element of tautology that obscures the meaning. It would make freedom the purpose of being set free. Our translation gives the true meaning, I think, since the exhortation is to stand fast in the freedom which Christ has given us. Christ died to purchase this liberty for us, among other purposes, and the apostle exhorts us to stand fast in that liberty and not be held again in the yoke of bondage to the legal restrictions of the ceremonial law. The only yoke that Christians are under is the love yoke which causes us to want to obey God's revealed will.

2. Trust in the Law Demands Complete Obedience to the Law (5:2,3)

a. **(5:2)** *"Behold, I, Paul, say to you, that if ye be circumcised Christ will be of no advantage to you."* Of course Paul is not saying that a person who is circumcised cannot be saved, for he himself was circumcised. What he is saying is that if we believe that faith in Christ is not sufficient to save a man, but that, for example, we must also be circumcised in order to be saved (or for that matter do anything else in order to be saved, such as keeping the seventh day Sabbath, or being immersed or something else) then we are again placing ourselves in bondage to the law, and Christ will not save us. "Their circumcision would be for them the sacrament of excision from Christ" (Pulpit Commentary). Accepting circumcision is "not only a useless imposition, a slavish burden; it is pernicious and fatal in itself" (Lightfoot).

b. **(5:3)** *"And I testify again to every man who receives circumcision that he is a debtor to keep the whole law."* Paul is making a solemn statement as a witness before Christ, that all

who think it necessary to be circumcised in order to be saved
are by that act assuming the burden of keeping the whole law
in every detail, for they are in effect saying that they want to
earn their own salvation by their law keeping. They cannot
possibly keep the law perfectly in every detail, so they are
cutting themselves off from salvation.

3. Trust in Law Severs from Christ (5:4)

(5:4) *"You have severed yourselves from Christ, whosoever of
you would be justified by the law; you are fallen away from
grace."* "You have severed yourselves" means that Christ has
become of no effect to you. That is, by trusting for salvation in
works of the law, you have placed yourselves in a realm where
the work of Christ is inoperative. The last clause, "you are
fallen away from grace," has been held by many to teach that a
person can be saved and then lose that salvation. This of course
would make Paul contradict himself, for he clearly teaches that
if a person is saved "nothing can separate him from the love
of God" (Romans 5:10; 8:39). In this verse Paul is apparently
teaching that a person who is trusting in legalism is ceasing to
trust in the grace of God. Such a person may never have been
born again, and so never saved, or if he has been born again,
he is lapsing into a state of sin that makes the grace of God
inoperative. It is sadly true that Christians at times turn their
backs on the sanctifying power of the Holy Spirit and so temporarily "fall from grace," so that God's grace is nullified in
their lives. If such a condition becomes permanent, then it
means that the apparent faith they had previously shown was
mere historical faith, not saving faith. If they are truly children
of God they will return to the grace of God in Christ alone.
Probably this happened (we trust) in the case of the Galatians
to whom Paul is writing.

4. Faith in Christ, Ground of Only Hope of Righteousness
(5:5,6)

a. (5:5) *"For we through the Spirit wait for the hope of
righteousness by faith."* In contrast Paul here says that true
Christians who trust in Christ alone, through the power of the
Holy Spirit patiently await the God-given righteousness to be
received by faith alone. It is a problem whether "by faith" is
to be connected with "righteousness" or with the verb "await."
The word order would seem to favor the connection with the
verb, as the Revised Versions connect it. However Paul's doc-.
trine of justification by faith alone would indicate that the con-

nection is with "righteousness" and that connection certainly makes better sense.

b. (5:6) *"For in Christ Jesus neither circumcision is of any avail nor uncircumcision, but faith working through love."* The force of "for" is to give a reason for the fact that Christians are waiting the hope of righteousness by faith. That reason is the knowledge that the condition of circumcision or uncircumcision makes no difference. What makes all the difference is whether there is genuine faith in Christ which is working in the life through the force of love. We show our faith when it works through love in our lives. Our physical conditions, circumcision or uncircumcision, being baptized or not being baptized, being immersed or being sprinkled, or any other conditions apart from faith, have no effect upon our salvation. That salvation is through faith in Christ alone. We are justified only through faith in Christ, not through what we do or do not do. We will, if we have true faith, show love for God and the brethren in our lives, but even that love is not the ground of our salvation and justification.

5. Temptation to Trust in Law Does Not Come from God (5:7,8)

a. (5:7) *"You were running well; who hindered you from obeying the truth?"* "The important lesson here for us all is that as long as we are obeying the truth we are getting along well; . . . The obedient child of God has joy and peace in Christian experience" (Lehman Strauss: *Devotional Studies in Galatians and Ephesians*). This expression from a race constitutes an appeal by Paul to the previous Christian life of the Galatians. He is praising them for their previous faith and seeking to recall it to their minds so that they will return to it. Paul knows very well who hindered them, so this is a rhetorical question.

b. (5:8) *"This persuasion is not from him who called you."* Their condition of disobedience to the truth is a temptation sent by Satan, not from God who called them. Satan worked through the Judaizers, giving them a mind to hearken to the false doctrine taught by the Judaizers. The Galatians had been deceived by Satan and now need to know that this new doctrine is not from God's Spirit but from the Evil One.

6. Compromise on a Little Point Will Destroy the Whole (5:9)

(5:9) *"A little leaven leavens the whole lump."* Leaven in the New Testament is almost always a symbol of evil. Leaven of course is yeast. The lump refers to the whole Galatian church. If a few of them depart from the truth at this point, the false doctrine will spread through the whole church is Paul's meaning. The only exception to the leaven being the symbol of evil is in the parable of Jesus, Matt. 13:33 and Luke 13:20,21.

7. Paul Trusts Them to Stand Firm (5:10)

(5:10) *"I have confidence in you through the Lord that you will take no other view than mine, and he who is troubling you shall bear the judgment, whoever he may be."* Perhaps Paul seems to be whistling to keep up his courage, but he has confidence that God will keep them true to the faith he has taught them. If they are God's own children, they are safe in God's care, and however they may stray away from the truth temporarily, Paul feels sure God will bring them back to the truth. The ones who are responsible for the defection, however, will have to bear their judgment from God. Probably there was some one in particular among the Judaizers who was largely responsible for their defection, and Paul has that person especially in mind.

8. Paul Is Not a Compromiser (5:11,12)

a. (5:11) *"But I, brethren, if I still preach circumcision, why am I still being persecuted? Then the offence of the cross hath been done away."* Possibly the Judaizers were charging that because Paul had circumcised Timothy he was still secretly teaching circumcision. Paul makes an argument "ad hominum" against them by pointing out that if that were true they would not have reason for persecuting him. If he were to compromise on the matter of circumcision, the message of the cross would no longer be an offense to the Jews, for it would imply that after all they were really Jews, not Christians, and should therefore be treated as Jews, since they believed that law keeping was necessary to salvation. But Paul is not compromising and therefore they continue to persecute him. It was the doctrine that belief in Christ's atonement alone was all that was necessary to salvation that was particularly offensive to the Jews and the cause of their persecution of Paul and the other Christians.

b. (5:12) *"Would that those who are troubling you would even mutilate themselves."* The interpretation that this is a wish on Paul's part that the Judaizers would separate or cut themselves off from the other Christians and let the Galatians alone is too weak as an explanation of the bitter wish of Paul regarding these Judaizers. The word *apokopsontai* in the context can hardly have such a transmuted ethical meaning. It is rather a reference to the practice among the Galatians at the city of Pessinus, where the worship of Cybele was carried on, of the priests castrating themselves. What Paul is saying is that since these Judaizers are urging circumcision, a useless self-mutilation, he wishes that they would go further and urge castration so that their foolishness would be self-evident!

B. Though the Christian Life Is One of Liberty, That Does Not Mean License (5:13-15)

1. The Law Is Fulfilled through Love of Neighbor as Oneself (5:13,14)

a. **(5:13)** *"For ye, brethren, were called unto freedom, only use not the freedom for an occasion to the flesh [i.e., for license] but through love serve ye one another."* Christians are called to liberty, not to bondage, as the Judaizers would have them be in bondage to the law. But that does not mean that they are free to serve the lusts of the flesh, as some of the antinomians would have it. We are saved by grace but we are saved to obey Christ, not to obey the devil. The Galatians want to be in bondage to something. Very well, be slaves to each other, bound with the bonds of holy love for the brethren. Possibly some of the Galatians were using their new found liberty to live sinful lives. Paul at once corrects any such false idea of liberty in the gospel. It is freedom to be holy.

b. **(5:14)** *"For the whole law is fulfilled in one word, even in this: Thou shalt love thy neighbor as thyself."* Love is the constraining principle in the Christian's life. Love for one's neighbor as oneself means (1) not to injure the neighbor in any way, and as far as is consistent with one's own safety and welfare, to prevent others from injuring the neighbor. This means that we are not to coerce our neighbor but are to allow him to pursue self-regarding interests as long as they do not injure others. It means that we are not to take our neighbor's wife. It means that we are not to take our neighbor's property (steal from him). It means that we are not to lie about him. It means that we are not to covet what rightfully belongs to him. Coveting means to long for or ardently desire that which belongs to another and to which we have no legal or moral right, and which we cannot obtain by legitimate means such as purchase or barter. (2) Love for one's neighbor means forbearance, that is, it means that we forgive his shortcomings and allow him the same freedom that we desire for ourselves. (3) Love means that we are to show him charity, helping him in sickness, injury or misfortune over which he has no control. It means helping him when oppressed by others. Such charity, however, is according to our own desire, not the desire of others. Love does *not* mean what the socialist and communist say it means: "from everyone according to his ability to everyone according to his need [or desire]." (4) Love means that we owe our neighbor the gospel.

(5) Love also means that we must have good-will toward our neighbor, or show a beneficent attitude toward him. Love does *not* mean that we must show him the affection we have for a wife or children or friends of our own choosing. We are not *compelled* to show such affection for anyone.

2. Quarrelling Destroys Both Parties (5:15)

(5:15) *"But if ye bite and devour one another, take heed that ye be not consumed one of another."* Christian freedom expresses itself in mutual love, so we must be on our guard lest we exploit each other or try to injure each other. If we do that we will be in danger of injuring ourselves as much as the other person, and of course will not be loving them as ourselves. When Christians quarrel they are injuring themselves.

C. The Christian Life Produces the Fruit of the Spirit (5:16-26)

1. The Spirit of God Is Contrary to the Lust of the Flesh (5:16-18)

a. **(5:16)** *"But I say, walk by the Spirit, and ye shall not fulfil the lust of the flesh."* This verse points back to verse 13 where he declares that we are not to use our freedom to fulfil the lusts of the flesh. We can obey this injunction by walking by the Spirit. The Spirit is of course the Holy Spirit, not the human spirit.

b. **(5:17)** *"For the flesh lusts against the Spirit, but the Spirit [fights] against the flesh; but these things are opposed to each other in order that you should not do the things that you want to do."* "The flesh" is of course the whole sinful nature, not merely the physical flesh of the body. This sinful nature lusts against the Holy Spirit, desiring ardently to do those things which the Holy Spirit disapproves. The indwelling Holy Spirit, however, fights against the sinful nature. These things thus are opposed to each other. There is, then, in the Christian's life, this continual battle between the sinful nature and the Holy Spirit dwelling in the Christian's heart. If a person wants to do the right, the flesh opposes it, while if one wants to follow the promptings of the sinful nature, the Holy Spirit fights against it. The purpose of this struggle is on both sides to prevent one from doing what he wants to do, as the last clause of the verse indicates. If one wants to do evil, the Holy Spirit opposes it, while if one wants to do good, the sinful nature opposes it. The fact of this struggle in the Christian's heart would be discouraging were it not that the Christian must take as his commander the Holy Spirit (verse 18).

c. **(5:18)** *"But if ye are led by the Spirit, ye are not under law."* Paul omits some of the steps in his argument, and leaps at once to his conclusion, namely, that the Christian is not in any sense bound by the law. The missing steps in Paul's argument are probably as follows: If we make the sovereign choice of following the Holy Spirit's promptings, then we will automatically oppose the desires of the flesh as the Holy Spirit wants us to do. If we make the choice of obeying the Spirit, we will do what is right freely, and not under the compulsion of the law. Thus the Christian who obeys the Spirit will not be under the condemnation of the law, since he will be doing right. And since he is doing right freely because he *wants* to obey the Holy Spirit, he is actually free from all the demands of the law. Walking by the Spirit (verse 16) is thus the key to the struggle (Rom. 7:15,16) that occurs in the Christian's heart.

2. The Works of the Flesh and the Fruit of the Spirit (5:19-24)

a. **(5:19)** *"Now the works of the flesh are plain, which are adultery, fornication, uncleanness, licentiousness."* "All sin is man's *work,* and it is fruitless of good (Eph. 5:11). All holiness is the *fruit* of the Spirit, the result of the new life which he implants" (Irwin). Paul does not enumerate all sins, but those into which the Galatian Christians in their environment would be most in danger of falling. "Adultery" is omitted in the Nestle text, and may be a gloss. Christians must always remember that they are not above temptations such as these here enumerated.

b. **(5:20)** *"Idolatry, sorcery, enmities, strife, jealousies, wraths, contentions, divisions, heresies."* These are only some of the sins that proceed out of the sinful heart of man.

c. **(5:21)** *"Envyings, murders, drunkennesses, revels, and things like these; of which I tell you beforehand, even as I also said before, that they who practise such things shall not inherit the kingdom of God."* Paul apparently refers to his visit to the Galatians on his previous journey. The word "practise" means habitual action as the rule of their life. This is no warrant, however, for indulging in these sins even one time. "The kingdom of God" here has its principal reference to future life after death.

d. (5:22) *"But the fruit of the Spirit is love, joy, peace, long-suffering, kindness, goodness, faith."* As a result of the new birth by the Spirit these Christian graces are the fruit. "The first three comprise Christian habits of mind in their more general aspect, 'love, joy, peace'; the second gives special qualities affecting a man's intercourse with his neighbor, 'long-suffering, kindness, beneficence'; while the third, again general in character like the first, exhibits the principles which guide a Christian's conduct, 'honesty, gentleness, temperance' " (Lightfoot). *Pistis,* "faith," here probably means "honesty" as Lightfoot translates it.

e. (5:23) *"Gentleness, temperance: against such things there is no law."* "Law exists for the purpose of restraint, but in the works of the Spirit there is nothing to restrain" (Lightfoot). The comments of Lehman Strauss, in *Devotional Studies in Galatians and Ephesians,* while too long to quote here, are excellent on these qualities in the Christian life. When a person is walking in the Spirit, the law has no connection with him as he wants to manifest these qualities.

f. (5:24) *"But they that are of Christ Jesus have crucified the flesh with its passions and lusts."* Those who are the slaves of Christ Jesus have crucified (aorist) the sinful nature both in principle in the crucifixion of Christ, and also at the time of conversion. The "passions and lusts" of the flesh refer to the passive and active expressions of the sinful nature.

3. A Life by the Spirit Demands a Walk by the Spirit (5:25,26)

a. (5:25) *"If we live by the Spirit we should also walk by the Spirit."* The first clause probably refers to the new birth, though it may refer to the whole Christian life under the sanctification by the Spirit. However there would be no reason for the last clause (which may be either "let us walk" or "we should walk") if we were already habitually living by the Spirit in daily life. The reference is thus probably to the new birth which was the source of our spiritual life. We are urged to reckon ourselves dead to sin and to walk daily led by the Spirit.

b. (5:26) *"Let us not become vain-glorious, provoking one another, envying each other."* Vain-glory, or conceit, must be guarded against for that produces anger in others. Nor should we envy others, either their spiritual qualities or their possessions.

D. The Christian Life Demands Mutual Helpfulness (6:1-5)
    While We Help Each Other as Christians Each Must Do His Part (6:1-5)

a. **(6:1)** *"Brethren, even if a man is overtaken in any trespass, ye who are spiritual restore such a one in a spirit of gentleness, considering yourself, lest you also be tempted."* The man in this verse is of course a Christian brother. Christians are a true brotherhood, because they are the true children of God. The Bible does not teach that all men are brothers in the intimate sense in which Christians are brothers. "Overtaken" means "detected" or "suddenly surprised" by others in the very act of committing a trespass. This word does not refer to "betrayed into sin," i.e., suddenly seduced by a gust of temptation. It refers to a trespass discovered by others in the very act. "Trespass" means a "transgression," that is, an external act of sin, a slipping off the high road of Christian living into the mire beside the road. The "spiritual" means those who are living lives led by the Spirit of God, obedient to his guidance. It is the duty of such mature Christians to show brotherly love to the sinning brother, and seek to restore him to the spiritual highway of obedience to the revealed will of God. But when such help is given it should be given, not with a spirit of self-righteousness and condescension, but in a spirit of meekness or gentleness, remembering that we are liable to succumb to the same temptations or similar ones. "Let him that thinketh he standeth, take heed lest he fall." Mutual helpfulness must be the quality of Christians, not censoriousness, or pharisaical "passing by on the other side."

b. **(6:2)** *"Bear ye one another's burdens, and thus fulfil the law of Christ."* In English it might seem that the burdens in this verse and the burden in verse 5 are the same and that there is a seeming contradiction. But in verse 2 the *bare* means "heavy burdens," too great for one to bear alone. We are urged to help such a one carry that heavy load by sympathetic help and seeking to restore the erring brother to the solid road of obedient Christian living. In verse 5 the burden is *phortion,* a "pack" just the right size for a man to carry. We must each bear our own packs of troubles. The law of Christ which we are to fulfil is the golden rule of love for brethren.

c. **(6:3)** *"For if a man thinketh himself to be something when*

he is nothing, he deceiveth himself." The connection of this
verse is with verse 1, giving a reason for treating the erring
brother gently. If we are proud of our spiritual attainments
and think we are fully capable of resisting temptation while we
are just as weak as our brother when we are tempted, we are
deceiving ourselves. If we think more highly of ourselves than
we ought to think (Rom. 12:3), we prove that we are nothing
in the sight of God. Self-deception about our ability and power
to resist temptation in our own strength is one of the common
sins of Christians. "Never look upon our erring brother as if he
were less spiritual than ourselves. The conceited man is a deceived man and is in no condition at all to restore a sinning
brother. . . . When a man has a high regard for his own moral
goodness he has a false estimate of himself" (Strauss).

d. **(6:4)** *"But let each one test his own work and then he shall
have rejoicing in himself alone and not unto another."* Here is
the rule for Christians in self-analysis: compare your work and
yourself this year with what you were previously, and if you
can see spiritual progress, then we can rejoice in our own
hearts, and not boast that we are better than other Christians.
When we see a fellow Christian fall into sin, it is easy to "thank
God that we are not as other men," as did the Pharisee in the
temple. We are to examine our own lives in the light of God's
word and see ourselves as God sees us.

e. **(6:5)** *"For each man shall bear his own burden."* The contrast with verse 2 is clear by the Greek words used. Here the
"burden," *phortion,* is really "pack" or "knapsack," and the
figure of speech is taken from the roll of blankets and clothes
which most travellers carried on their backs. Every Christian
has his own temptations and anxieties, his own weaknesses and
problems. He must face them squarely and bear the burdens he
is called upon to bear. The heavy load of defeat and failure
implied in "bearing each other's heavy loads" should be shared
by fellow Christians who sympathize, help and encourage those
who have had a failure.

E. The Christian Life Demands Liberality (6:6-10)

1. If We Have Learned, We Are Obligated to Support the
Teacher (6:6)

(6:6) *"But let him that is taught in the word share with him
who teaches, in all good things."* Verse 5 might be taken by the
readers as justification for refusing to help financially their
religious teachers, if each man is to bear his own burdens, so

Paul rectifies this by laying down the principle that the laborer is worthy of his hire (I Tim. 5:18). A religious teacher should be supported by those whom he teaches if he is giving full time to the work. However this verse goes beyond the teaching of such financial support for teachers of religion. The "sharing in all good things" implies the responsibility of sharing in the work of proclaiming the gospel truth. Christians are taught Christian truths, and therefore have the responsibility for teaching others those truths.

2. We Reap What We Sow (6:7-10)

a. **(6:7)** *"Be not misled; God is not mocked; whatsoever a man soweth, that also he shall reap."* "What? You still hold back? Nay, do not deceive yourselves. Your niggardliness will find you out. You cannot cheat God by your fair professions. You cannot mock *Him.* According as you sow, thus will you reap" (Lightfoot). The connection with the preceding verse is this: selfishness is a sin of Christians as well as the sin of unbelievers. A wealthy farmer who was adding to his bank account every year, was deeply stirred by the sermon of his pastor on stewardship. He talked the matter over with his wife and then spoke to the pastor and told him: "Preacher, my wife and I are convicted of not giving what we ought to the work of the Lord, so this year we are going to increase our giving by 100%! Last year we gave fifty cents each for the year and this year we are going to give $1.00 a year each!" Apparently Paul thought the Galatian Christians had an idea like that, so he told them that they could not deceive God by withholding their financial support to their religious teachers. That would be mocking God. If they wanted to receive good spiritual things from their teachers they must give sacrificially, or they would dry up spiritually through their own excessive selfishness.

b. **(6:8)** *"Because he that soweth to his own flesh shall of the flesh reap corruption, but he that sows to the Spirit, from the Spirit shall reap life eternal."* "If you plant the seed of your own selfish desires, if you sow the field of the flesh, then when you gather in your harvest, you will find the ears blighted and rotten. But if you sow the good ground of the Spirit, you will of that good ground gather the golden grain of life eternal" (Lightfoot). This paraphrase of Lightfoot's sets forth the teaching of this paragraph. The flesh is the sinful desires of the sinful nature. This is both the seed and the soil. If selfish Christians withhold the tithe due to the Lord's work, nothing they do will be untainted with their selfishness. "We are God's stewards, and as such we will reap a harvest in proportion to our sowing" (Strauss). Of course we are not to get the idea that eternal life will be the reward of faithful stewardship of our property. That would be getting the cart before the horse. If we understand the principles of Scriptural stewardship, as born-again Christians we will want to be faithful stewards, and that will be the mark of those who have life eternal.

c. (6:9) *"But we should not be discouraged in well-doing, for in due time we shall reap if we faint not."* When anything is planted, the sower must learn patience, one of the hardest Christian virtues to cultivate. Impatience with the slowness of the growth of the seed planted is one of the greatest temptations of the gardener. The same thing is true in the Christian life. As we look at ourselves in self-analysis, it is easy to be discouraged at the lack of progress we seem to have made in Christian living. But we have the promise of the Lord that we shall reap if we have patience and endure to the end. Paul generalizes in this verse, dwelling upon the figure of the sower and the seed. Sanctification is a gradual growth, not a sudden gift of the Spirit. Let us never think that because our financial generosity is not suddenly rewarded by tangible spiritual results, no results will ever be forthcoming. In God's own time he will give the harvest of spiritual blessings if we do not faint. In Hebrews 12:3, 5 the word for "fainting," *ekluomenoi,* is used of giving in morally, and that is probably the thought here. If we do not give in to temptation to live unto the flesh, God will see to it that in his own time we will reap spiritual blessings.

d. (6:10) *"So, then as we have opportunity, we should do good towards all men, but especially towards them that are of the household of the faith."* Here in this verse the apostle raises his eyes to the horizon and encompasses in his gaze the farthest reach of mankind. The Christian should not only aid and comfort those who are of the household of the faith, but should extend his generosity and charity to the other side of the earth. All men, everywhere, are included in this generous sweep of the apostle's love. Christians have always been the first to engage in famine relief or in the relief of the needs of refugees. Christians have founded hospitals and orphanages for the relief of human suffering everywhere. Care for the lepers of the earth has been the task of Christian charity long before governments began to take over such work. Such wide-spread charity is the duty of all Christians. But while all this is true, the primary responsibility is for the care of those who are fellow-Christians, "of the house-hold of the faith." We must never forget that we have an intimate, personal responsibility for needy Christians that ex-tends far beyond our responsibility for the underprivileged classes in other nations, or for the poverty-stricken unbelievers in this land. All Christians belong to the household of God, and we should feel differently toward the needs of Christian brothers than we do toward the needs of unbelievers. If there is not enough money to help all men, the needy among our Christian brethren must be cared for first out of the benevo-lences of Christians. It is all very well to give to cancer research, red cross, heart disease research, and mental health campaigns, but for Christians these causes should not occupy the major part of our benevolent giving. We must never neglect the poor and needy among our Christian brethren.

With this verse the main part of the Epistle to the Galatians comes to a close. The rest of this chapter covers the conclusion of the epistle.

CONCLUSION (6:11-18)

A. Paul's Own Handwriting (6:11)

(6:11) *"See with what large letters I am writing to you with my own hand."* Paul at this point takes the pen from the hand of the amanuensis and begins to write in large characters with his own hand.

B. Those Who Would Compel Circumcision Are Not Sincere, for They Do Not Keep the Law Themselves (6:12,13)

1. (6:12) *"As many as wish to make a good showing in the flesh, these compel you to be circumcised, only in order that they may not be persecuted for the cross of Christ."* The real reason the Judaizers were trying to force the Galatian Christians to be circumcised was that they themselves might escape the persecution that came to those who trusted only in the cross of Christ for salvation. All such people were anxious to make a good reputation as being zealous for the keeping of the law. If they could compel the Galatians to be circumcised, then they could point to them as evidence of their zeal for keeping the Mosaic law, and so escape persecution. "In the flesh" probably means "in external rites." Believing in Christ was not the particular stumbling block with the Jews. It was advocating the abandonment of the rites of the ceremonial law that was the real stumbling block. Circumcision was the supreme rite that set the Jews off from other people. Making proselytes of the Gentiles by forcing them to undergo circumcision was the outward proof of keeping the law.

2. (6:13) *"For they who are being circumcised do not keep the law; but they wish you to be circumcised, in order that they may boast about your flesh [lit. in your flesh]."* Paul makes the further charge of insincerity against the Judaizers. Though they were themselves circumcised, they did not keep the other requirements of the law of Moses, but were seeking to compel the Galatians to be circumcised in order to have something to boast about to the other non-Christian Jews. Not only was the distance from Jerusalem preventing them from offering the sacrifices required by the law; they had no personal zeal for rigorous law observance themselves. "Sarki," "flesh," here is to be taken literally as referring to the rite of circumcision itself. Probably

Paul had received special information about the Judaizers and
their lack of rigorous law keeping as the basis for his attacks
upon them here. It seems more likely that they were converted
Jews rather than converted proselytes.

C. Paul's Glory Is in the Cross of Christ Alone (6:14)

(6:14) *"But as for me, God forbid [lit. may it not be] that I
should glory except in the cross of our Lord Jesus Christ,
through whom the world has been crucified to me, and I to the
world."* In his use of the word "cross" here, Paul does not mean
primarily the wooden beams of the cross, but the crucifixion of
Christ on the cross in place of his people. This is the only thing
that Paul boasts about. While the Judaizers tried to cling to the
old associations of the law and its ceremonies, and therefore to
boast about their keeping the law, Paul has given all that up
when he put his trust in Christ as his Saviour. Through Christ
Paul has severed all earthly ties that are implied in all that he
had given up: his ancestral privileges, his pharisaical privileges,
and Jewish friends and relatives. He nailed these, and all that
pertained to that world, to the cross with Christ, so that they
are dead to him and he is dead to them. The *kosmos* here is
the specific social and political and economic world of Paul as
a Jew.

D. Circumcision and Uncircumcision Are Not Important, but
a New Creature (6:15)

(6:15) *"For in Christ Jesus neither circumcision nor uncircumcision is of any force, but a new creation."* (We have followed the Textus Receptus in this verse rather than the neutral
text, which omits *Christo Iesou* and *ischuei*, and inserts the *en.
Estin* is omitted in the Textus Receptus.) The reason why Paul
glories in Christ and his cross is that to all those who believe
in Christ it makes not a particle of difference whether they are
circumcised or uncircumcised as far as their ground of salvation
is concerned. That ground is the atoning work of Christ on the
cross, and they will be saved if they trust in that work alone.
No wonder he can boast in Christ and his cross! The all-important thing is that the believer is a new creation in Christ. "Old
things have passed away." If a man is born again into the kingdom of Christ, then nothing else really matters. Only if one
puts his faith in circumcision does it become important whether
he is circumcised or not. Paul could circumcise Timothy because it really did not matter and would avoid Jewish criticism,
since neither Timothy nor Paul believed the rite had any

efficacy, but when the Judaizers insisted that the Galatians should be circumcised in order to be saved, that put the matter in an entirely different light and called forth this epistle with its condemnation of the Judaizers. The all-important thing is that we shall be new creatures in Christ, and become dead to the world and alive to Christ and his will.

E. Paul Blesses Those Who Walk by This Rule (6:16)

(6:16) *"Let peace and mercy be upon all those who walk by this rule, and upon the Israel of God."* The "rule," or "line," refers primarily to a carpenter's rule or a surveyor's line, and then is taken over into religion as the rule of life. But to what does he refer as the "rule"? Some would refer this back to verse 14, glorying only in Christ as the rule of life. Others would refer it back to the whole rule of trust in Christ alone for salvation, set forth throughout the epistle. We believe that in the light of the original word order it would seem to point to what had immediately preceded, namely, putting the new creation as the all-important thing in the Christian life, that is, living as a new creature in obedience to the golden rule of Christ and trusting only in his atoning work for salvation. Peace and mercy are besought for all such. "And upon the Israel of God" refers back to the statement Paul made in Gal. 3:29, "And if ye are Christ's, then are ye Abraham's seed, heirs according to promise." All true believers are the true Israel. Upon this true Israel of God Paul invokes the blessing.

F. Paul Bears the Marks of Jesus (6:17)

(6:17) *"Henceforth let no one trouble me; for I bear the brands of the Lord Jesus in my body."* "St. Paul closes the epistle, as he had begun it, with an uncompromising assertion of his office: 'Henceforth let no man question my authority: let no man thwart or annoy me. Jesus is my Master, my Protector. His brand is stamped on my body. I bear this badge of an honorable servitude' " (Lightfoot) . "The brands" were placed on slaves to indicate ownership. Paul belongs to Jesus and has these brands on his body and soul. But what are the brands? Probably they are the scars of the beatings he received in persecutions. Certainly they are not the "stigmata" of the Roman Catholic Church. Such stigmata were marks on the palms and on the feet similar to the holes caused by the nails in Christ's hands and feet on the cross.

G. Benediction (6:18)

(6:18) *"The grace of our Lord Jesus Christ be with your spirit, brethren. Amen."* Paul has a note of tenderness in this concluding benediction. It is a prayer that the Galatians may have the indwelling gracious presence of our Lord Jesus Christ in their hearts (spirits). The *Amen* at the close is an attestation of Paul's sincerity and earnestness. He calls them "brethren" as a touch of love for them and to show that he has not cast them off no matter what great sin they may have committed.